符号中国 SIGNS OF CHINA

中国扇

CHINESE FANS

"符号中国"编写组 ◎ 编著

中央民族大学出版社
China Minzu University Press

图书在版编目(CIP)数据

中国扇：汉文、英文／"符号中国"编写组编著. —北京：
中央民族大学出版社，2024.3
（符号中国）
ISBN 978-7-5660-2278-3

Ⅰ.①中⋯ Ⅱ.①符⋯ Ⅲ.①扇—介绍—中国—汉、英 Ⅳ.①K875.2

中国国家版本馆CIP数据核字（2024）第016762号

符号中国：中国扇 CHINESE FANS

编　　著	"符号中国"编写组
策划编辑	沙　平
责任编辑	舒　松
英文指导	李瑞清
英文编辑	邱　械
美术编辑	曹　娜　郑亚超　洪　涛
出版发行	中央民族大学出版社
	北京市海淀区中关村南大街27号　　邮编：100081
	电话：（010）68472815（发行部）　传真：（010）68933757（发行部）
	（010）68932218（总编室）　　　　（010）68932447（办公室）
经 销 者	全国各地新华书店
印 刷 厂	北京兴星伟业印刷有限公司
开　　本	787 mm×1092 mm　1/16　印张：10.25
字　　数	133千字
版　　次	2024年3月第1版　2024年3月第1次印刷
书　　号	ISBN 978-7-5660-2278-3
定　　价	58.00元

版权所有　侵权必究

"符号中国"丛书编委会

唐兰东　巴哈提　杨国华　孟靖朝　赵秀琴

本册编写者

易　凡

前言 Preface

扇子，是日常生活中用于扇风祛暑的工具，但是当人们将丰富的文化内涵赋予它以后，一把普通的扇子就变得丰富多彩起来。

中国是世界上最早使用扇子的国家。扇子在中国不仅种类丰富，而且功能多样。王侯将相，凭借高大的仪仗扇显示皇室的威严；文人墨客，在方寸之间的扇面上挥毫泼墨；普通的百姓则

Fans are used in daily life as a tool to generate a cooling breeze and provide relief from heat. Fans have also become a rich and colorful representation of Chinese culture and art.

China has the earliest record of fan usage in the world. There are a wide variety of Chinese fans for different functions. Kings and court officials demonstrated their power with tall and huge ceremonial fans. Literati showed their literary talents by writing and painting on small fans. Common people sat chatting under the shade of a tree with a palm-leaf fan in hand. A small hand fan has recorded five thousand years of Chinese civilization.

会手摇一把芭蕉扇，在树荫下闲聊家常……一柄小小的扇子，记录了中华五千年的文明。

本书从中国古代最古老的扇子着手，梳理了扇子在中国的发展流变，展示了各种扇子独有的魅力，并通过扇子在其他领域的运用，让人们对中国古代的扇子有一个更为全面的了解。

This book explains the evolution and changes of Chinese fans starting from the oldest fans to the unique style of different types of fans and their applications in the Chinese history. The book is intended to provide a comprehensive understanding about ancient Chinese fans.

目 录 Contents

扇之韵
Charms of Fans 001

扇子的起源
The Origin of Fans 002

扇子的流变
Evolution of Fans 011

扇之美
Beauty of Fans 027

竹扇
Bamboo Fans 028

羽扇
Feather Fans 032

团扇
Round Fans 037

折扇
Folding Fans 047

蒲葵扇
Chinese Palm Leaf Fans 063

1

檀香扇
Sandalwood Fans 070

象牙扇
Ivory Fans 074

其他扇子
Other Fans 077

扇之雅
Elegance of Fans 087

扇子与书法绘画
Fans with Calligraphies and Paintings 088

扇子与诗词小说
Fans in Poetry and Novels 104

扇子与戏曲曲艺
Fans in Chinese Operas
and Traditional Art Forms of Quyi 117

扇子与舞蹈
Fans in Dances 129

扇子与园林建筑
Fans in Landscape Architecture 139

扇子与民俗礼仪
Fans in Folk Customs and Etiquettes 145

扇之韵
Charms of Fans

中国是世界上最早发明扇子的国家，扇子在中国已经有三千多年的历史。关于扇子的起源，民间流传着许多动人的传说故事；历经数千年的演变而流传下来的扇子，更是为人们的生活增添了无尽的风采。

China is the first country in the world to invent fans. Fans in China have over three thousand years of history. There are many beautiful legends and folktales about the origin of fans. After thousands of years of evolution, Chinese fans have also added tremendous delights to people's life.

> 扇子的起源

关于扇子的起源，中国民间流传着女娲"结草为扇"的传说。据唐代李冗《独异志》记载：远在盘古开天辟地的时候，天下只有伏羲、女娲兄妹二人。为了能够使人类繁衍生息，兄妹俩商议决定要结为夫妻。但这毕竟有悖于伦理，于是他们便爬到了昆仑山顶向天祷告："如果上天同意我们兄妹结为夫妻，就让天上飘着的几朵白云聚为一团。"话音刚落，那几个云团便渐渐移近，聚合成了一团。于是，女娲与伏羲便结成了夫妻。成婚当晚，女娲因为害羞，就用蒲草编织了一把扇子挡住自己的脸。这就是民间流传的"羲扇"的由来。传说古时候举行婚礼时，新娘头上蒙着的红盖头就是源于伏羲与女娲

> The Origin of Fans

One of the many legends about the origin of fans is the story of Nvwa and Fuxi. According to *Strange Anecdotes* by Li Rong, Tang Dynasty (618-907), before Pangu creating the universe there were a brother (Fuxi) and a sister (Nvwa) living in the Kunlun Mountain. In order to reproduce mankind they decided to become husband and wife. But that would be a breach of ethics, so they climbed up to the top of the mountain and prayed, "If the heaven allows us to be husband and wife, please let clouds gather together."Upon their prayer, the clouds slowly came together and became one. When they got married that night, Nvwa was very shy and covered her face with a fan she made from cattail leaves. This fan became the legendary "*Xi* Fan" named after Fuxi. It is said that red veils

- 《伏羲女娲图》

  伏羲女娲上身相拥，下身蛇尾相交。伏羲手持矩，女娲手持规，代表天圆地方。

  Fuxi and Nvwa

  In the painting, Fuxi and Nvwa embrace each other in their upper bodies with snake-like lower bodies intertwined. Fuxi holds a square representing the earth and Nvwa holds a compass representing the sky.

结婚时使用的羲扇。

　　还有一个传说是"舜帝造扇"。据晋人崔豹《古今注》中记载：舜为了能广泛听取民意，曾制作"五明扇"。"五"代表东、西、南、北、中五个方向，"五明"即广达圣明。传说这是一种用雉鸡的羽毛做成的扇子，舜帝在巡

used by Chinese brides to cover their faces in ancient Chinese weddings were originated from *Xi* Fan used by Nvwa and Fuxi when they get married.

　　Emperor Shun's fan was another legend about the origin of fans. According to *Interpretations of Ancient and Current Events* by Cui Bao of the Jin Dynasty (265-420), Emperor Shun invented the Sage Fan of Five Directions for his plan to get good ideas from people. Five directions were the east, west, south, north and center. The name of the fan was a eulogy for the emperor's wisdom and graciousness. It is said that this fan was made of pheasant feathers and used by Emperor Shun during his

幸各地时，沿途用"五明扇"来作为招纳贤人的标志。

很显然，上面的两个传说故事是后人为教化民众而刻意编造的，其实扇子的发明是一个自然而然的

inspections around the country as a sign of recruiting talents.

These legends were probably make believe. The invention of fans has its own natural development. In the primitive

- **《孔子圣迹图》焦秉贞（清）**
  此画描绘的是孔子游说诸侯的故事。孔子是春秋时期的一位思想家，面对当时诸侯纷争的局面，他主张以德治国，为宣传自己的政治主张而周游列国。
  画中席地而坐的是孔子，坐在他对面红木椅子上的是一位诸侯。诸侯的后面站有五个随从，其中有两个人手中拿着长柄的仪仗用扇。

  Painting of the Sacred Footprints of Saint Confucius by Jiao bingzhen, Qing Dynasty (1616-1911)
  The painting describes how Confucius lobbied among kings. Confucius was a thinker during the Spring and Autumn Period (770 B.C.-476 B.C.) and Warring States Period (475 B.C.-221 B.C.). Facing various disputes among kings of different states, he strongly advocated his theory of running the government through rites and morality. In order to promote his political beliefs he started lobbying everywhere.
  In the painting Confucius sits on the mat talking to a king on the redwood chair. Behind the king are five of his servants, among whom two hold long-handled ceremonial fans.

盘古开天地的故事

传说太古时候，天地不分，整个宇宙像一个鸡蛋，混沌一团。但鸡蛋中孕育着一个伟大的人物，他就是盘古。盘古在鸡蛋中足足睡了一万八千年，有一天他终于从沉睡中醒来。醒来之后他看到四周一片漆黑，很是憋闷，便抓起一把大斧，用力一挥，只听得一声巨响，鸡蛋骤然破裂，其中类似蛋清的东西向上不断飘升，变成了天，而沉重的类似蛋黄的东西渐渐下沉，变成了大地。

天地分开以后，盘古害怕天地又会合拢，他就用头顶住天，用脚踏住地，站在天地之间。他每天增高一丈，天也随之升高一丈，地也随之增厚一丈。就这样过了一万八千年，天地终于稳固了，而盘古也累得倒在了地上。临死之前，他呼出了最后一口气，后来变成了风和云；他最后发出的声音变成了雷电；他的四肢变成了大地的四极；他的血液变成了江河；他的左眼变成了太阳，他的右眼变成了月亮；他的头发和胡须变成了星星；他的皮肤和汗毛化作花草树木，牙齿骨头化作金银铜铁、玉石宝藏；他的汗变成了雨水和甘露……从此便有了世界。

The Legend of Pangu Creating the Universe

It is said that in the prehistoric times there was no sky or earth except a chaos embedded in the world like a huge egg. A great man named Pangu had slept inside the egg for eighteen thousand years. One day he woke up and saw nothing but darkness everywhere that made him feel stuffy. He swung his giant ax and broke the huge egg open with a loud noise. The thing like the egg white floated up and became the sky. The heavier egg yolk sank and turned into earth.

After he separated the sky and the earth, Pangu was afraid that they would merge into one again. So he stood between them with his feet on the earth and head pushing up the sky. Each day he grew ten feet taller with the sky becoming ten feet higher and the earth ten feet thicker. After eighteen thousand years the sky and the earth were finally stabilized. Pangu was so tired that he fell to the ground dead. His last breath became wind and cloud; his last voice became the thunder; his arms and legs formed the east, west, north and south of the earth; his blood turned into rivers, his left eye the sun, his right eye the moon, and his hair and beard stars; his skin and body hair became trees, flowers and grass; his teeth and bones changed to gold, silver, copper, steel and jade; his sweat fell as rain and morning dews. Hence the universe was born.

过程。原始社会，先民在炎炎烈日下劳作，自然会想找某些东西来遮阳取凉。一开始，人们会以多种不同的东西来扇风，但是久而久之，就会发现其中的某一样特别合适。于是这件物事便被固定下来专门用来扇风，也就意味着最原始的扇子诞生了。再后来，随着人类文明的进步，人们在原始扇子的基础上加以改造，使其更为美观，这就产生了后世各式各样的扇子。

society, people worked under the scotching sun and would find something to cover or cool themselves. In the beginning, they used different things to generate cooling breezes. After a long time of experiments one thing was found to be the most effective and people began to use it all the time to generate breezes, which brought about the original version of fans. With the progress in civilization people started to transform the primitive version into fans of beautiful appearances and wide varieties.

• 精美的折扇
Exquisite Folding Fan

扇子的别称

在古代，扇子有很多别称。扇子产生初期，被称为"箑"（shà）或是"翣"（shà），这与早期扇子多用竹子和羽毛制作有关。

魏晋时期，扇子又有了一个"扬仁风"的雅号。传说这与当时的宰相谢安有关。有一年，谢安的朋友袁宏要去外地做官，临别前，谢安就送了一把扇子给他。聪明的袁宏立刻明白了他的意思，于是说："我到任之后，一定廉洁公正，弘扬仁义之风。"从此以后，人们便给了扇子一个"扬仁风"的雅号。

从功能上着眼，人们还给了扇子"凉友""招风"这样的雅号。宋代陶谷《清异录·器具》中引："诗云：'净君扫浮尘，凉友招清

Other Names of Fans

In ancient times, fans had many other names. In the very beginning, they were called "sha", which was mostly related to early fans made from bamboo and feathers.

In the Wei and Jin dynasties, fans got a graceful name of Fanning Benevolence Breeze. It is said that Yuan Hong, a friend of Xie An, was about to take office in another place. Xie An was the prime minister at the time. Before his departure, Xie An gave him a fan as a gift. The smart Yuan Hong immediately understood the implication of the fan and said, "When I take office, I will uphold integrity and fairness fanning the breeze of benevolence." From then on, people gave fans this elegant name.

Based on the practical function, people also gave fans nice names such as

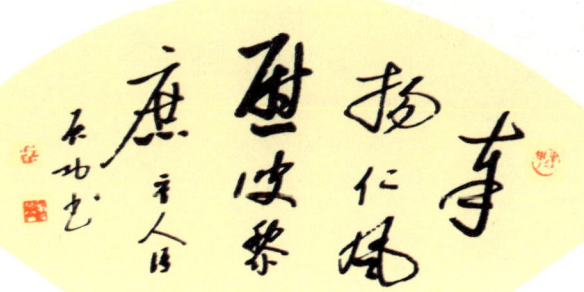

- 启功书法扇面
  Calligraphy Fan Leaf by Qi Gong (1912-2005)

• 木雕折扇
Folding Wood-carved Fan

风。'"诗中以"净君"代指扫帚,"凉友"代指扇子,文雅得体。

具体到不同类型的扇子,也会有不同的别称。例如,团扇有"纨扇""宫扇""合欢扇""便面""障面"等多种称呼。其中有很多称呼是源自诗词。例如,西汉班婕妤作《团扇诗》:"裁为合欢扇,团团似明月。"于是,团扇就有了"合欢扇"的别称。唐代诗人王建《调笑令》中有:"团扇,团扇,美人并来遮面。"由此又衍生出"便面""障面"的雅

a Cooling Friend or Breeze Generactor. According to his notes about utensils, Tao Gu in the Song Dynasty (960-1279) quoted a poem that said "The cleaning man sweeps away dust and the cooling friend induces a breeze." The cleaning man refers to the broom and the cooling friend means the fan, which is very well put.

Different types of fans had different names. For example, round fans were called fine silk fans, court fans, happy reunion fans, a face cover or a hand screen. Some of these names came from poems. Ban Jieyu in the West Han Dynasty (206 B.C.- 25 A.D.) wrote this verse in her poem *Ode of Round Fans* : "Cut silk into a happy reunion fan, so round like the bright moon." Then Happy Reunion Fan became a name for round fans. Wang Jian, a poet of the Tang Dynasty wrote in his poem, "Round fan, round fan, a beauty uses one to cover her face." This poem brought about the name of "face cover" for round fans.

• 象牙镂空团扇
Pierced Round Ivory Fan

号来。

明、清两代颇为流行的折扇，在当时有"怀袖雅物"的别称。"怀袖"，是说它小巧，开合方便。"雅物"是因为文人在扇面上题诗作画，使它带有了浓厚的文学色彩。

Folding fans became very popular in the Ming (1368-1644) and Qing (1616-1911) dynasties. They were given the name "an elegant ornament in the sleeve". "In the sleeve" indicates that folding fans are small and easy to open and close. "An elegant ornament" refers to the poetry and paintings on the fan leaf by scholars and artists of literary taste.

• **精美的折扇**
Exquisite Folding Fan

扇业祖师——齐纨

杭州市内兴忠巷有座扇业祖师殿，殿内供奉的祖师叫"齐纨"。殿内除主要供奉齐纨外，还供有六百多位扇业艺人的牌位。但是这座祖师殿始建于何时已经无从考证。

齐纨，历史上并没有这个人，可能是因为西周时期一种名叫"齐纨"的细绢与制作扇子有关而被误认为是人物。

齐纨是古时候齐国出产的一种细绢，它与当时鲁国出产的一种生绢"鲁缟"，并称"鲁缟齐纨"。齐纨是制作扇面的重要原料，而后世又称细绢制成的团扇为"纨扇"，大概由此，与扇子有关的细绢"齐纨"便被附会为扇子的创始者，从而被奉为扇业祖师。

Qi Wan, Founder of Fan Industry

There is a temple in memory of Qi Wan, the founder of the fan industry in Xingzhong Street, Hangzhou City. In addition to Qi Wan, memorial tablets for over six hundred fan craftsmen were placed in the temple. However, no historical record was found to trace back when this temple was built.

There is actually no such person named Qi Wan in history. In the Western Zhou Dynasty (1046 B.C.-771 B.C.) there was a type of fine silk called *Qiwan* used in making fans. Therefore, it could have been mistaken as a person's name.

Qiwan was a kind of white fine silk produced in the State of Qi. Together with a raw silk called *Lugao* from the State of Lu, they were referred to as *Lugao* and *Qiwan*. Qi Wan was a very important raw material for making fan leaves. Later people called round fans made from white fine silk Wan fans. Probably this was how Qi Wan became the name of the fan industry founder.

> 扇子的流变

中国古代的扇子从功能上讲分为两种。一种是仪仗用扇，一种是生活用扇。

仪仗用扇，又称"障扇"，最初是帝王或王室成员外出时，用来遮挡阳光和灰尘的用具，后来逐渐演变成一种显示皇室威仪的工具。仪仗用扇，一般多为长方形，扇面用羽毛或竹篾编织而成，有一个长长的扇柄在下面，供他人在后面执握。唐代画家阎立本所绘《步辇图》中，宫女手中所持的两把长柄大扇就属于仪仗用扇。

仪仗用扇产生的时间很早。西周时期的周武王就曾用雉鸡的羽毛做成障扇，并规定了不同等级的官员用扇的标准。唐朝，改用孔雀羽毛代替雉鸡羽毛做成仪仗扇，当时

> Evolution of Fans

In ancient China fans were divided into two types according to diffcrent functions. One was ceremonial and the other was for daily and personal use.

Ceremonial fans, also known as "fan screens" were originally used for emperors and the imperial families to cover them from sunshine and dust when they went out. They gradually evolved into decorations for the imperial court to demonstrate their power and majesty. Ceremonial fans usually were in a rectangular shape. The fan leaf was made of feathers or woven with bamboo strips supported by a very long handle held by the fan-bearer. The famous *Painting of Imperial* Carriage by Yan Liben in the Tang Dynasty shows two ceremonial fans with very long handles held by two court maids.

● 《步辇图》阎立本（唐）

该画描绘了唐太宗李世民接见吐蕃使臣的情景。唐太宗端坐在由六名宫女抬着的步辇上，两名手持仗扇的宫女立在他身后。画中的李世民舒眉朗目，体现出封建帝王的自信与威严。李世民对面站着三个人，其中身穿红袍的是引荐官，中间穿着少数民族服饰的便是吐蕃的使者，后面穿白衣服的是翻译官。

Painting of Imperial Carriage by Yan Liben, Tang Dynasty (618-907)

This painting shows Li Shimin, Emperor Taizong of Tang meeting an envoy from Tibet. The emperor sits on a sedan chair carried by six court maids with additional two standing behind him holding ceremonial fans. Li has a confident and dignified look. Standing before him are three people among whom one in red robe is the referrer official, one in ethnic clothing the Tibetan envoy and one interpreter in white cloths standing in the back.

称之为"凤尾扇"，并制定了"索扇"制度，以此来进一步增强皇帝的威严。"索扇"制度是唐玄宗时期的宰相萧嵩提出来的。所谓的"索扇"，与现在戏剧舞台上幕布的功能很相似，就是皇帝每次走上大殿之前，都先用扇子遮挡一下，等皇帝坐定之后，再将扇子移去，当皇帝退朝时，也要用扇子遮挡一下。这样做的目的是拉开皇帝与大臣的距离，以此来加强皇帝的威

Ceremonial fans came into being as early as in the Western Zhou Dynasty (1046 B.C.-771 B.C.) when King Wu had fan screens made of pheasant feathers. King Wu also established rules to design fans according to the ranks and positions of court officials. In the Tang Dynasty pheasant feathers were replaced by peacock feathers for ceremonial fans known as "Phoenix Tail Fans" at the time. Xiao Song, a minister for Emperor Xuanzong of the Tang Dynasty proposed

- 《杨贵妃上马图》【局部】钱选（元）
  在杨贵妃身后有两名手拿长柄仪仗扇的侍从。画面中可以清晰地看到扇面上绘制的凤凰图案。
  Painting of Imperial Concubine Yang Guifei Riding a Horse (Partial) by Qian Xuan, Yuan Dynasty (1206-1368)
  Behind Concubine Yang stand two servants holding long-handled ceremonial fans with painted phoenix patterns.

严，维护皇权的稳定。仪仗用扇自产生之初，一直到明、清时期，凡是有王公贵族出行的场合，都会有障扇出现。

　　宋代以后，民间传统的婚嫁仪式中也开始使用仪仗扇，但是在规格和形制上，与皇家用扇还是有很大区别。传说这一习俗与宋徽宗有关。宋徽宗在位期间，骄奢淫逸，民间怨声载道。为了平复民怨，他便下令允许民间在婚礼上使用只有皇族才能使用的仪仗扇。此后一直到民国时期，百姓结婚都会使用仪仗扇来壮大声势。

a court rule of using fans as curtains to strengthen the solemnness of the emperor. A curtain fan had the same function as a stage curtain. When the emperor walked to his seat in the palace hall, a curtain fan was placed to block him from being seen. When he sat down on his seat, the fan was moved away. When the emperor was leaving, the curtain fan was used again. The purpose was to widen the distance between the emperor and his ministers and maintain the stability of the imperial power. Ever since their appearance, ceremonial fans had been used all the way to the Ming and Qing dynasties. Whenever the imperial family and nobles came out fan screens were used to block

• 现代人展示的老北京满族婚俗，画面中可见到两柄黄色的龙凤掌扇。

The painting shows a present-day performance of an old-fashioned wedding ceremony of Manchu people in Beijing with two yellow palm-shaped ceremonial fans painted with dragon and phoenix.

仪仗用扇，更多的是一种身份的象征，实用价值并不大。日常生活中，人们普遍使用的还是一些轻巧简便的生活用扇。

较早的生活用扇中有一种叫作"便面"的扇子，较为流行。"便面"出现于战国后期，是用竹篾编织成的，扇面多为长方形或梯形，在扇面的一侧安有一个木质扇柄。

them from being seen by the public.

After the Song Dynasty (960-1279) ceremonial fans were also used in the traditional weddings for the common people. But the style and application were quite different from those of the imperial court. It is said that this tradition was related to Emperor Huizong of the Song Dynasty. During his reign, Emperor Huizong led an extravagant and dissipated life, which caused widespread disgruntlement among his people. In order to calm down people's discontent, he ordered to let common people use ceremonial fans of the imperial court in their weddings. Since then, ceremonial fans became common in ordinary people's weddings to make them look grandeur and this practice was continued to the Minguo Period (1912-1949).

Ceremonial fans are mostly a symbol of social status with very little value in their functionality practical function. Hand fans on the other hand are widely used in people's daily life because they are light and convenient.

An earlier type of personal fans was used as hand screens, which were quite popular in the late Warring States Period. Hand screen fans were made from woven bamboo strips. The shapes

· 湖南长沙马王堆汉墓出土的短柄竹扇
(图片提供：FOTOE)
A Short-handled Bamboo Fan Unearthed in the Mawangdui Archaeological Site in Changsha, Hunan Province

因为形状近似于房间的门扇，所以也有"单门扇"之称。与仪仗用扇不同，这种"便面"的扇面比较小，扇柄也比较短，使用起来也更为灵活方便。所以自"便面"出现一直到两汉时期，上至帝王将相下至黎民百姓都在使用，使用范围相当广泛。

除了竹篾编织的"便面"之外，在早期的生活用扇中还有一种用羽毛制成的扇子也比较普遍。最初的羽扇是用鸟类的半个翅膀做成的，后来人们也将鸟的羽毛攒在一起做成扇子，这便是最早的羽扇。中国有史料记载的最早的羽扇，是西周时期的丹鹊羽扇。据晋代王嘉《拾遗记》记载：西周时期曾有涂修国进献丹鹊鸟给周昭王。当夏季到来丹鹊鸟开始换毛时，昭王便命

of the fan leaves were either rectangular or trapezoid. On one side of the fan leaf a wooden stick was installed. Because the shape of the leaf looked like a door, this type of fans was also called "single door" fans. Compared with ceremonial fans, hand screen fans had much smaller leaves and shorter sticks, which made them easy to carry. They became very popular till the Han Dynasty (206 B.C.-220 A.D.), both among the emperors and nobles as well as common people.

In addition to the bamboo woven hand screens, another type of personal fans made of feathers were also quite common in ancient times. In the very beginning, half of the bird's wing was used to make a feather fan. Later people learned to gather feathers to make fans. The earliest historical record shows that feather fans were made from red sparrow

• 《消夏图》刘贯道（元）
画中一位士大夫模样的人舒适地斜倚在床榻上，在他前面是两位侍女，其中一位侍女手中拿一把长柄团扇。

Painting of Away from the Summer Heat by Liu Guandao, Yuan Dynasty (1206–1368)
In the painting, a scholar official leans comfortably on a daybed with two maids standing in front of him, one holding a long-handled round fan.

人收集这些羽毛，将其制成四把扇子。这时刚好东瓯国献来两个美女，一个叫延娟，一个叫延娱。昭王吩咐这两位美人专职摇那几把大扇子，扇子一摇，顿时能感到阵阵凉风。

春秋战国时期，羽扇已经开始在南方地区使用。西晋统一全国之后，有南方的人士到当时的都城洛阳做官，于是便将羽扇由南方带入中原地区。一开始，北方人看到南方人手持羽扇便嘲笑他们，但是在南方著名的文人陆机发表了一篇论述羽扇之美的文章之后，北方人逐渐改变了对羽扇的态度。

到了南北朝时期，随着羽扇制作工艺的日益提高，精巧雅致的羽扇在上流社会普遍流行。帝王用它来赏赐大臣，朋友之间也经常用

feathers. The book Memoir on Neglected Stories by Wang Jia in the Jin Dynasty (265-420) said that in the West Zhou Dynasty, State Tuxiu offered a tribute of a red sparrow to King Zhao of Zhou, who then asked people to gather all the features from it and make four fans. At the same time State Dong'ou offered a tribute of two beautiful girls, one named Yanjuan and one named Yanyu. King Zhao asked them to wave the big fans on either side of him all day long to get cool breeze.

In the Spring and Autumn Period and the Warring States Period, the use of

羽扇纶巾

这个成语的意思是：手中摇着羽扇，头上戴着青丝带做的头巾，形容一个人镇定、从容。这个成语出自宋代文人苏轼的词《念奴娇·赤壁怀古》。他用这个词来形容三国时期的大将周瑜在赤壁之战中指挥若定的样子。

实际上，魏晋时期的许多名士都是这种装扮。南朝的陶弘景就经常手拿羽扇，头戴纶巾。他隐居在山中，皇帝几次派人去请他出来做官，他都不同意。后来皇帝就经常派人去山里面请教他，人们都称他为"山中宰相"。

Feather Fan and Green Scarf

The Chinese idiom "Feather Fan and Green Scarf" describes a person's calmness state of mind. It came from a verse *In Memory of the Battle of Chibi* by Su Shi, a famous poet of the Song Dynasty (960-1279), in which he used these words to describe the calmness of General Zhou Yu in commanding the battle.

Actually many celebrities in the Wei and Jin dynasties dressed up with accessories of a feather fan and a green scarf. One of them was Tao Hongjing in the Southern dynasties who had a seclusive life in the mountains and rejected multiple offers from the emperor to come out and be an imperial court official. The emperor had to go into the mountains personally to ask him for advice. Therefore people called him the "minister in the mountains".

- 《隐士高逸图》孙位（唐）

该画描绘的是魏晋时期的四位名士——山涛、王戎、刘伶、阮籍。他们是一群放荡不羁的文人，喜欢聚在一起对一些哲理性的问题进行论辩。画面中他们分别坐在华丽的地毯上，每人旁边都有一个小童侍候。其中抱膝而坐的是山涛，手拿如意的是王戎，手执羽扇的是阮籍，低头看酒杯的是刘伶。图画将不同人物的个性特色和清高、傲慢、放荡不羁的精神状态都刻画得恰如其分。

Painting of Literary Recluses by Sun Wei, Tang Dynasty (618-907)

The painting describes four well-known scholars in the Wei and Jin dynasties: Shan Tao, Wang Rong, Liu Ling and Ruan Ji. They were a group of indulgent literati, who liked to get together to debate on philosophical issues. In the painting, they all sit on a gorgeous carpet, each served by a young servant. Shan Tao sits with his knees tucked in; Wang Rong holds a Ruyi scepter; Ruan Ji has a feather fan; Liu Ling looks down at his wine. The painting depicts vividly their aloof, arrogant and untamed personalities.

- 京剧表演中手拿羽扇的诸葛亮
Peking Opera Character Zhuge Liang with His Feather Fan

羽扇作为互相馈赠的礼物。当时的许多文人也作文章来赞美羽扇。古典名著《三国演义》中的人物诸葛亮，就经常是以手拿羽扇的形象出现。以至于后来，羽扇也被看成是一种智慧、儒雅的象征。

隋、唐时期，随着纺织技术的进一步发展，团扇代之而起，成为扇子中的主流。团扇扇面多为圆形或椭圆形，与月圆时的明月很相似，故此得名。又因为其扇面材质多为纨、绢等丝织品，故也被称作"纨扇"。目前所见的最早的团扇实物是新疆阿斯塔那唐代古墓中出土的木柄绢制团扇。实际上早在西汉时期团扇就已经出现，但由于两晋时期，国家曾严格提倡节俭，两

feather fans started to spread to the south. After China was unified in the Western Jin Dynasty, people from the south began to take official positions in Luoyang, the capital of Jin. They brought feather fans from the south to central China. At first, the northerners laughed at the southerners who carried hand fans made of feathers. Lu Ji, a well-known scholar at the time from the south took the opportunity to write an essay about the beauty of feather fans, which changed the attitude of the northerners towards feather fans.

In the Southern and Northern dynasties (420-589), craftsmanship in making feather fans had increasingly improved. Elegantly and exquisitely made feather fans became very popular among the upper class. The emperors and kings bestowed fans on their ministers as rewards. People gave them to friends as gifts. Literati wrote articles to praise fans. In the famous Chinese classic *the Romance of the Three Kingdoms*, Zhuge Liang, a key character in the novel, always appeared with a feather fan in his hand. As a result, feather fans became a symbol of wisdom and refinement.

With further development in the textile technology, round fans started to emerge and became the main stream

- 新疆吐鲁番阿斯塔那唐代古墓出土的长柄绢质团扇 （图片提供：FOTOE）
A Long-handled Round Silk Fan Unearthed from an Ancient Tomb of the Tang Dynasty (618-907) in Astana, Turpan of Xinjiang

- 《韩熙载夜宴图》【局部】顾闳中（南唐）
画面中韩熙载手拿团扇
Painting of Han Xizai's Night Life (Partial) by Gu Hongzhong, Southern Tang Dynasty   Han Xizai carries a round fan in his hand.

度明令禁止使用团扇，所以团扇没有流行开来，一直到唐宋时期才得以真正流行。

in fan making during the Sui and Tang dynasties. The fan leaves were mostly round or oval looking very much like the full moon. A full moon represents reunion, which in Chinese is pronounced *"Tuanyuan"*. So came the name for round fans (*"Tuanshan"* in Chinese). Most raw materials used for round fan leaves were fine silk (*"Wan"* in Chinese) and spun silk, hence another name *"Wanshan"* for round fans. The earliest round fan was discovered in the ancient tomb of the Tang Dynasty in the Astana area of Xinjiang. Round fans in fact first appeared in the Western Han Dynasty (206 B.C. -25 A.D.). However, due to frugality strictly enforced by the imperial court, round fans were banned twice in the Jin Dynasty. Therefore, it did not become popular until the Tang and Song dynasties.

中国团扇在日本

　　团扇在奈良时代由唐朝传入日本，最初只在宫廷中使用，是一种身份的象征。一直到平安时代末期，团扇才被允许为普通百姓使用；江户时代后期，团扇的使用开始普及；到了元禄时代，团扇已经成为日本女子不可或缺的配饰。

　　就团扇形状而言，日本团扇保留了唐代团扇以圆形为主的特点。但是在功能上，传入日本的团扇发生了很大变化。在日本，团扇不仅是扇风取凉的工具，还代表着一种宗教文化信仰。如遇到战争，武士们会带上一把扇面上绘有日月、星辰的团扇作为临战指挥的工具。最早相扑裁判使用的工具也是一把团扇。

Chinese Round Fans in Japan

Chinese round fans were introduced to Japan in the Tang Dynasty (618-907) during the Japanese Nara Period. In the beginning they were only used in the palace as a symbol of one's social status. Common people were not allowed to use them until the Heian Period. In the late Edo Period round fans started to spread among common people. In the Genroku Era round fans became an indispensable accessory for Japanese women.

　　Japanese round fans maintained the round shape of the Tang Dynasty fans. But the functions had changed a lot. In Japan a round fan was not only used as a tool to get a cooling breeze, but also represented Japanese religious and cultural beliefs. During times of war Japanese warriors would carry a round fan painted with the sun, moon and stars as a commanding tool. Round fans were even used by the referees in the early Japanese wrestling matches.

● 日本浮世绘中手拿团扇的美人 (图片提供：FOTOE)
A Women Holding a Round Fan in a Japanese Woodblock Print

- 手持团扇的女子
  Woman Holding a Round Fan

受古代封建礼教的束缚，古代的女性是不能在公众场合抛头露面的，尤其是未出嫁的女子。但是她们也有好奇心，也有到外面走走的需要。团扇的出现很好地解决了困扰她们的问题。一把团扇在手，既避免了被人看见的尴尬，又形成了一种犹抱琵琶半遮面的美感，一举两得。

两宋时期团扇依然是扇子当中的主流，但是一种形制新颖的折扇也开始出现，它最初是日本使者进献的礼品。折扇的出现，在形状、材质上都是对团扇的突破。折扇可以折叠，携带方便，扇面材质也改用纸张做成。由于数量有限，在

In ancient times restrained by the feudal proprieties, women were not allowed to reveal their faces in public, especially for unmarried women. Out of curiosity for the outside world, they had to go out sometimes and round fans solved this problem for them. Using a round fan to cover the face, they avoided the awkwardness of being seen entirely by men, and were also able to show partially their hidden beauty.

In the Song dynasties (960-1279) round fans were still the mainstream, and a new type of folding fans also emerged. They were tributes to Chinese emperors offered by Japanese envoys. Folding fans were a breakthrough from the traditional round fans in both the shape and materials used. These fans could be folded and were easy to carry. Paper was used to make fan leaves. Because only a limited number of these folding fans were brought to China at the time, only upper class people were able to obtain them. According to historical records, Su Zhe, brother of the famous Song poet Su Shi was thrilled to receive a Japanese folding fan as a gift.

In the Southern Song Dynasty, fan makers tried to replicate the Japanese folding fans. Due to immature techniques,

• 折扇——红梅吐秀
Folding Fan with Plum Flower Painting

当时只有上流社会的人才能使用折扇。史料记载，苏轼的弟弟苏辙曾经因为得到一柄他人赠送的日本折扇而兴奋不已。

南宋以后，中国制扇工匠开始仿制这种折扇，但是由于工艺上还不成熟，仿制的折扇很粗糙。但仆役们喜欢折扇灵活方便、便于携

the products were not that exquisite. But servants liked their portability. Whenever they had a short break they would use the folding fan to get some breeze. As soon as they were called by their master, they would fold the fan and insert it right back into their belts. Therefore folding fans at the time were also called "waist fans".

Folding fans were widely used in the Ming and Qing dynasties. Emperor Zhu Di of the Ming Dynasty was very fond of folding fans for its portability and that it was easy to fold and unfold. He ordered his craftsmen to make them in large quantities, and painted with his poems and paintings. He then rewarded his ministers with these fans, which promoted the popularity of folding fans at the time. In the Qing Dynasty people began to use folding fans even more frequently. As a result, the price for folding fans started to go up. It cost a lot of money to buy a beautifully crafted folding fan. Besides

• 折扇
A Folding Fan

带的特点，空闲时抽出折扇扇风祛暑，遇到主人呼唤就立刻将扇子折上插入腰间，所以在当时折扇也被称为"腰扇"。

折扇的广泛使用是在明、清时期。由于明成祖朱棣喜欢折扇开合自由、携带方便的特点，便命令工匠大量制作折扇，并在扇面上题诗作画，分赠给众大臣，一时间折扇流行开来。到了清代，折扇的使用更加频繁。由于人们对折扇的喜爱，也促使其价格逐渐上涨，当时得到一把制作精美的扇子要花费很多钱，而且每个人还要备有几十把扇子，扇子已经成为一张名片，折射出一个人的经济实力与文化水准。

折扇一旦流行，便久盛不衰。人们不但用它扇风祛暑，还将其雅致美观的特点加以发挥，制作出巨大的挂扇作为室内的装饰用品。2008年中国举办奥运会期间，奥运会组委会将印有"中国印"的扇子作为礼物，送给前来观看奥运会开幕式的各国元首，这既体现了中国作为礼仪之邦所具有的美德，又充分展示了中国悠久的历史文化。

除了以上介绍的几种扇子之外，勤劳智慧的中国人民还创制出

people used to have dozens of folding fans with them, which resembled today's business cards, showing the person's financial and cultural status.

The popularity of folding fans has never died down. Hand folding fans have been extended from getting cool airflow to huge and elegant hanging fans as interior decorations. In 2008 when China hosted Summer Olympic Games, the Olympic Committee gave all heads of states attending the opening ceremony fans printed with the Chinese seal as its official gifts. These fans demonstrated the long history of Chinese culture and Chinese people's hospitality as a host county.

In addition to the fans introduced above, the Chinese people also invented

• 清代山水、人物、书法泥金折扇
Gilded Folding Fan with Landscape, Figures and Calligraphy of the Qing Dynasty (1616-1911)

• 清代八大山人扇面
Fan Leaf Painting by Zhu Da, Qing Dynasty(1616-1911)

• 清代俞樾隶书扇面
Fan Leaf with Clerical Script Calligraphy by Yu Yue, Qing Dynasty (1616-1911)

了檀香扇、象牙扇、蒲葵扇、麦秸扇、兽皮扇等一系列扇子，而且将审美情趣渗透到扇子当中，创造出了扇面书画、题扇诗等多种形态的文化艺术表现形式。

sandalwood fans, Chinese palm leaf fans, wheat straw fans and animal skin fans, etc. Chinese fans embody artistry and aesthetics by various art forms such as calligraphies and paintings on fans.

中国折扇在欧洲的传播

中国折扇精致高雅，到了明朝，折扇经由葡萄牙人之手传入了欧洲。中国折扇进入欧洲之后，深受欧洲人的喜爱，尤其是宫廷贵妇。在当时包括维多利亚女王在内的英国王室成员，都是有名的"扇子迷"。据史料记载，在清朝乾隆时期，广州的商人就曾专门生产过一批出口欧洲的象牙折扇。当时为了迎合欧洲人的喜好，他们还将象牙扇骨进行了精雕细刻，并在上面绘制了彩绘。

17世纪，欧洲的很多城市开始生产折扇，而且还能根据自身的喜好对中国折扇加以改造，将玳瑁雕刻镂空作为扇骨的装饰；有的还镶嵌上珍珠；为了与带有蕾丝的晚礼服相搭配，还制造出了带有蕾丝风格的扇子，从而使得折扇的装饰日渐高贵华丽。

到了18世纪，扇子在欧洲已经被视为时尚的象征。当时在出席晚宴的时候，女性都以手执一把极具东方情趣的折扇为骄傲。甚至连法国作家伏尔泰都说："不拿扇子的女士犹如不拿剑的男子。"可见扇子在当时之流行。

● 清代广州出口的黑漆描金开光折扇 (图片提供：FOTOE)
Black Lacquer Gilded Folding Fan Exported from Guangzhou in the Qing Dynasty (1616-1911)

Chinese Folding Fans in Europe

The Chinese folding fans are elegant and delicate. In the Ming Dynasty (1368-1644) Chinese folding fans were brought into Europe through the Portuguese and they were well-liked by Europeans, especially European court ladies. Members of the royal family in England including Queen Victoria were well-known enthusiasts of fans.

According to historical records merchants from Guangzhou particularly made a batch of ivory Brisé fans to export to Europe during Emperor Qianlong's reign in the Qing Dynasty. In order to match the European style, ivory fan sticks were exquisitely carved and beautifully painted.

In the 17th century many European cities started production of folding fans and redesigned them to satisfy the European taste. European brisé fans were made with carved or fretted tortoiseshell and some were even inlaid with pearls. There were also lace style fans to match lace evening dresses. Decorations on folding fans became increasingly splendid and fashionable.

In the 18th century, fans were considered a symbol of fashion. Women were proud to show up in dinner parties with a folding fan with an oriental style in their hands. Even the well-known French writer Voltaire said that "Ladies without a folding fan are like a gentleman without a sword", which shows the popularity of folding fans at that time.

• 《拿扇子的妇人》迭戈·德·席尔瓦·委拉斯开兹（西班牙） (图片提供：FOTOE)
Woman with a Fan by Diego Rodríguez de Silvay Velázquez, Spain

扇之美
Beauty of Fans

  中华民族善于发现美和创造美，即使是在日常生活中，也懂得将实用性与审美结合起来，这体现在扇子的创制上也不例外。人们赋予扇子多变的形态，用多种材质来丰富扇面，再加之精湛的工艺，呈现出一个丰富多彩的扇子世界。

Excelled in arts and crafts, the Chinese people combine the utility and anesthetics in things they use in their daily life. The innovation in fans is no exception. Chinese fans not only have a great variety of styles with fan leaves made of different types of materials, but also superb craftsmanship constructing a colorful world of art by itself.

> 竹扇

在扇子的发展史上，竹扇是出现较早的一种，至今仍为人们所用。编制竹扇所选用的竹子有：毛竹、慈竹、淡竹、水竹等。竹扇的形状有圆形、桃形、荷叶形等多种。根据编织时所用竹片的粗细，竹扇可分为"竹篾扇"和"竹丝

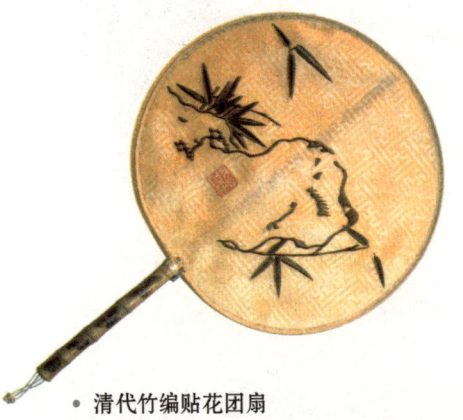

• 清代竹编贴花团扇
Round Bamboo Woven Floral Collage Fan of the Qing Dynasty (1616-1911)

> Bamboo Fans

In the history of fans, bamboo fans are one of the earliest known Chinese fans and people have been using them ever since it was invented. Bamboos used in weaving include moso bamboo, sinocalamus bamboo, henon bamboo and water bamboo. Bamboo fans are usually shaped like round, peach and lotus leaf. There are two types of bamboo fans depending on the thickness of bamboo strips used. The craftwork of weaving fans with thick bamboo strips is relatively simple. This type of bamboo fans is manufactured in most of the provinces in south China. They are well-liked among ordinary people because they are durable and inexpensive. The other type of bamboo fans is made from bamboo filaments and it is considered one of the four most famous types of fans in China.

- 清代竹编暗花团扇
  Bamboo Woven Round Fan with Implicit Floral Patterns of the Qing Dynasty (1616-1911)

扇"。"竹篾扇"是选用较粗的竹片，用基本的编织方法制作而成，制作工艺相对简单，中国南方的大部分省份都有生产。由于竹篾扇经久耐用，价廉物美，是普通百姓的首选。作为中国四大名扇之一的"竹丝扇"，是要将竹片劈成精细的竹丝，然后还要编出精美的图案，工艺相对复杂。四川自贡出产的"龚扇"为竹丝扇中的上品。

除了用竹篾编织成扇之外，还有一种用特殊工艺制成的竹扇——

The craftsmanship is more sophisticated with exquisite woven patterns made from delicate bamboo filaments. Gong fans from Zigong city, Sichuan province are the best of bamboo filament fans.

Another type of bamboo fans is called "Jade Board Fans", which uses large moso bamboos as the raw material and a special crafting technique. A small section (5-6 inches wide and one foot long) of the bamboo is cut off with its outer skin peeled off. Then this small piece of bamboo is boiled in the water

029

扇之美
Beauty of Fans

龚扇

"龚扇"因其创始人龚爵伍的姓氏而得名。据说龚爵伍当年原本是在自贡挑煤，由于当地天气炎热，就放弃了挑煤转而编起了扇子。由于他手艺精湛，编织的竹扇十分畅销。清末光绪年间，龚扇还被当作贡品选送进皇宫。光绪皇帝被其绝妙的工艺所折服，亲自赐名"宫扇"，从此以后龚扇声名远扬。

龚扇的原料，要采用四川特有的一年生青慈竹，最好取山阴处的慈竹，叶小、节长且没有斑点疤痕，在白露、秋分时节采伐最佳。竹材经清水浸渍之后，还要用刀子反复刮，刨去青皮，劈成竹篾，将竹篾剖得细如发丝一般，然后再将图案编制于扇面之上。通常一把成扇需要经过成百上千根竹丝的穿梭才能完成。龚扇扇面轻薄如蝉翼，柔滑似绸绫。正面对着阳光看，扇面呈现白色，图案花纹朦胧可见；向左侧视，花纹闪青色，树叶现白色；向右侧视，花纹现白色，树叶闪青色，真令人叹为观止。

Gong Fans

Gong fans were named after their founder Gong Juewu. It is said that Gong Juewu gave up his first job as a coal carrier and started to make fans because the local weather was too hot. Because of his high-quality craftsmanship, his bamboo filament fans were sold very well. By the end of the Qing Dynasty Gong fans were selected as a tribute for the emperor. Emperor Guangxu was so impressed by Gong's superb craftwork that he personally named them "Court Fans". After that Gong fans became famous all over the country.

Gong fans are made from green sino-calamus bamboos, a special local product of Sichuan province. The best sino-calamus bamboos grow in the shades with small leaves, long internodes and not any scars or spots. They are harvested around the Chinese solar terms of "white dew" and "autumnal equinox" in September. After soaked in the water, they are cut into bamboo strips from which bamboo filaments as delicate as silk are obtained. Patterns woven on a fan leaf require thousands of bamboo filament yarns. The Gong fan is very light and silky smooth. When it is put in front of the sunlight, white, but hazy patterns on the fan leaf can be seen through. When it is viewed from the left the floral patterns are green while tree-leaf patterns are white. When it is viewed from the right, the floral patterns are white while tree-leaf patterns are green. It is indeed an amazing craftwork.

• 龚扇第四代传人——龚道勇编织的《箜篌图》团扇
Round Fan Woven with *A Painting of Konghou* (a Chinese Musical Instrument) by Gong Daoyong, the Fourth Generation of the Gong Fan Makers

• 清代"王勋"款玉版扇
Jade Board Fan by Wang Xun, Master of Bamboo Carving of the Qing Dynasty (1616-1911)

玉版扇。玉版扇又称"竹簧扇",是选用大型楠竹为原料,从上面截取宽五六寸、长约一尺的一段,将其外皮剥离,之后经水煮、熨烫使其平整为竹版,最后再用红木、玳瑁为柄装成扇。因其颜色润白如玉,故称之为"玉版扇"。玉版扇形状如手掌,上宽下窄,可以两面雕刻书画,颇为雅致。

and ironed flat into a very thin bamboo board used as the fan leaf. A redwood or tortoiseshell handle is added to the fan. Because the leaf' color is as white as jade, it gets the name "Jade Board Fan". A jade board fan has a shape of a hand palm with a wider upper part and narrower lower part, and it is easy to carve paintings and poems on both sides.

> 羽扇

羽扇是经选用禽类的羽毛制作而成。羽扇在选材上很广泛，仙鹤、天鹅、孔雀、白鹭、大雁、雕、鹰、鸡、鹅、鸭的羽毛都可以作为制扇材料。

羽扇由扇面和扇柄两部分组成，以长方形居多。扇柄位于扇面

• 棕榈树下的白鹅
White Geese under a Palm Tree

> Feather Fans

Feather fans are made of bird feathers including feathers from cranes, swans, falcons, eagles, geese, egrets, chickens and ducks.

A feather fan consists of two parts: a leaf and a handle. Most feather fans are in a rectangular shape with the handle below inserted from the bottom to the center. The handle is usually made of wood or bamboo. High fashion fans use ivory and jade handles. Feathers are symmetrically arranged around the handle in the center and bamboo strips or metallic wires thread through the quills to tie them neatly together. Depending on size the of the feathers, a finished product can have ten or more feathers.

The process of making feather fans goes through many steps including collecting, selecting, brushing, washing,

的下部，居中，一般为木、竹材质，高档的羽扇会选择象牙、玉石。扇面以扇柄为中心，两边用羽毛对称排列，最后再用竹签或金属丝穿翎管编排成形。根据羽毛的大小，一把成品扇所用羽毛从十几根到数十根不等。

羽扇的制作要经过采羽、选

repairing and sowing feathers as well as installing handles and decorating with down feathers. Feather arrangement must be symmetrical on both sides. Feathers must be taken from the same position of either side of the bird's body to be able to have a symmetrical alignment on the fan leaf.

The value of a feather fan is decided by the type of feathers used. Goose and falcon feathers are the most common types. Goose feather fans are made of white goose quills and have round, oblong, heart or Buddha hand shapes. Each feather is less than 8-9 inches long.

● 羽扇 （图片提供：FOTOE）
Feather Fan

● 手拿羽扇的女子
Woman Holding a Feather Fan

羽、刷羽、洗羽、理毛、修片、缝片、装柄、整排、饰绒等诸多工序。凡制作羽扇，羽片排列必须两边对称，一般只能在一只禽鸟身上拔取左右两翼的同一位置的翎毛来配对成型。

根据所用羽毛的不同，羽扇的品类高下也有很大差异。常见的羽扇中以鹅毛扇与雕翎扇为最多。鹅毛扇以白鹅翎羽制成，有圆形、腰圆形、鸡心形、佛手形等。每羽长不足八九寸，一般用羽十至四十片不等。历史上著名的军事家诸葛亮手中拿的就是鹅毛扇。正因为如此，民间也称羽扇为"孔明扇"。

雕翎扇是用乌雕的羽毛做成的。乌雕又名花雕，全身呈褐色，体型巨大，性情凶猛，常栖息在草原及湿地附近的林地里，生活在中国东北、华北、华东、中南及新疆地区。雕翎扇外形美观、古朴，深受人们的喜爱。

浙江湖州自古以来就是羽扇的产地。湖州羽扇以质软风柔、毛片平薄、式样精美而著称。由于湖州羽扇扇出的风柔和，特别适宜老、弱、病人及孕妇使用，因此还有"产妇扇"的美誉。

Each fan uses about ten to forty feathers. The famous military strategist Zhuge Liang (courtesy name Kongming) in the Chinese history always had a goose feather fan in his hand. Therefore goose feather fans are also known as Kongming fans.

Falcon quill fans are made from feathers of spotted eagles, which are a large bird of prey in a very dark brown color with a ferocious temperament. Their habitat is in the woods close to wetlands and grasslands in northeast, north, east, and south central of regions China as well as in Xinjiang. Falcon feather fans are very well-liked by people for their simple and classic style.

Huzhou in Zhejiang province has always been the place to produce feather fans since ancient times. Huzhou fans are well known for its soft material, light weight and exquisite styles. They are especially good for the elderly, the sick and pregnant women because the breeze generated is very gentle. Thus Huzhou fans are also known as a "pregnant woman fan".

There is an interesting story about the softness of Huzhou fans. Once one of the Eight Immortals Lv Dongbin was selling glutinous rice dumplings under

● 湖州羽扇
Feather Fan of Huzhou

湖州羽毛之所以这么柔软，其中还有一个有趣的故事。传说"八仙"之一的吕洞宾曾在湖州城内骆驼桥下卖汤团。他用古桥下面的水煮制汤圆，其味鲜美可口。此后，制扇艺人也专取骆驼桥下的水来洗刷羽毛，洗后的羽片色泽光亮，毛质柔韧。当然这仅仅是个传说故事，不过湖州城内为苕溪所流经，而苕溪发源于天目山，水质好却是真实的，故用其洗刷过的羽毛会柔软而富有光泽。

the Camel Bridge in Huzhou. He used the water under the bridge to boil them and the dumplings came out with a delicious taste. Later fan craftsmen followed his example and washed feathers with water under the same bridge. The washed feathers became shining and soft. This is only a legend. In reality a river called Tiaoxi runs through the city of Huzhou and its water comes from the Tianmu Mountain. Thanks to the good quality of the water, feathers indeed turn shining and soft after being washed in the water from the Tiaoxi River.

中国古代"八仙"的传说

"八仙"是指中国民间传说中的八位神仙——铁拐李、汉钟离、蓝采和、张果老、何仙姑、吕洞宾、韩湘子、曹国舅。他们好打抱不平,惩恶扬善。

民间流传着许多关于他们的故事,最著名的就是"八仙过海"。故事说有一天,八位神仙一起到了东海,只见海面上波涛汹涌,巨浪滔天。这时吕洞宾建议说,大家不要乘船过海,要用各自的神通过海。于是其他诸位仙人都响应吕洞宾的建议,将随身法宝投于水面,然后立在法宝之上,乘风逐浪而过。后来,民间就有了"八仙过海,各显神通"的一句俗语,比喻那些依靠自己的过人能力而创造奇迹的人。

Legend of the Eight Immortals in Ancient China

The Eight Immortals in the Chinese folklore are: Tieguai Li, Han Zhongli, Lan Caihe, Zhang Guolao, He Xiangu, Lv Dongbin, Han Xiangzi and Cao Guojiu. They were Chinese vigilantes always defending the weak against injustice and punishing the evil to promote kindness.

There are many folk tales about them. The most famous one is the story of the Eight Immortals Crossing the Sea. One day the Eight Immortals came to the East Sea and saw extremely rough and turbulent waves. Lv Dongbin proposed that each immortal crosses the sea using his or her own magical power instead of taking a boat. Everybody agreed. They threw their own magic onto the sea and crossed the stormy East Sea successfully by riding on the magic. Later, the story became a Chinese proverb "the Eight Immortals cross the sea and each reveals its divine power", which describes those people who can overcome difficulties with his or her own special skills to create miracles.

- 《八仙过海图》
Eight Immortals Crossing the Sea

> 团扇

团扇由扇面、扇框、扇柄三部分组成，有时为了美观往往会在扇柄下面装饰上扇坠。团扇形状如满月，暗合中国人合欢、吉祥之意，所以自西汉定型一直到明清时期，团扇一直都深受人们的喜爱。

- 清代迦南木贴制团扇
  Round Canaan-wood Floral Collage Fan of the Qing Dynasty (1616-1911)

> Round Fans

A round fan is composed of the leaf, the frame and the handle. Sometimes a pendant or tassels with a netsuke is added below the handle as a decoration. The round fan has a shape of a full moon implying happiness of reunion and auspiciousness. The round shape was set in the Western Han Dynasty (206 B.C.-25 A.D.). From then on till the Ming and Qing dynasties, round fans were always very well-liked.

New materials, techniques and styles were introduced in making round fans. The appearance of round fans broke through the traditional rectangular or square shapes of feather and bamboo fans. Round fan leaves used different materials such as white fine silk, spun silk, gauze and aya silk fabrics, etc. With the development in papermaking

• 清代象牙团扇
Round Ivory Fan of the Qing Dynasty (1616-1911)

团扇的出现打破了以往羽扇、竹扇的形制，在材质、工艺、审美等方面不断推陈出新。在形状上，团扇扇面多为圆形，改变了之前扇面以方形为主的情况，让人耳目一新。在扇面材质的选择上，团扇也与之前的扇子不同，它多是使用纨、绢、纱、绫罗等丝织品。到了唐代，随着造纸技术的进步，以纸作为扇面的纸团扇也开始出现。

扇坠的使用也是团扇工艺的一个创举。宋代以后扇坠开始流行，明代以后，折扇也普遍开始配有扇坠。扇子配上扇坠之后，整体上使扇子的形状变得修长，增加了扇子的飘逸感。

早期的团扇多为单层扇面，到了明清时期才开始流行双层扇面。双层扇面是由一大一小两个紧密套在一起的圆形扇框组成的，很像今

techniques in the Tang Dynasty (618-907), paper round fans started to emerge.

Fan pendants and tassels were another invention for round fans. They started to get popular in the Song Dynasty (960-1279). After the Ming Dynasty (1368-1644) it was very common to see a folding fan with a pendant or tassels, which expanded the length of the fan adding a floating elegance.

Early round fans were mostly single-layered. In the Ming and Qing dynasties double-layered fans became popular. A double-layered fan leaf consists of two leaves stretched between two tightly clasped round hoops (one small and one big) similar to the hoops used in Chinese embroidery.

Calligraphies, paintings and Chinese traditional embroidery can all be applied to silk fan leaves. Embroidery techniques consummated in the Tang and Song dynasties with manifestations of flowers, birds, insects, fish, landscapes

天刺绣时使用的绣绷。

　　丝质的团扇扇面除了可在其上书写绘画之外，还能将中国传统的刺绣工艺运用其上。唐宋时期，刺绣工艺精湛，花鸟、虫鱼、山and portraits on fan leaves. In the Ming Dynasty, round fans began to use well-known paintings of the Song and Yuan dynasties as blueprints for embroidery. By combining painting and embroidery, the finished product was brought to life on the fan leave. The famous Gu

- 双面绣团扇扇面
  Round Fan Leaf with Double-Sided Embroidery

- 《团扇清歌仕女图》张大千（近代）
  Painting of Qing Court Lady with Her Round Fan by Zhang Daqian, Modern

顾绣

顾绣，是指明、清时期上海顾名世家族所作的刺绣作品。顾名世是明朝嘉靖年间的进士，晚年居住在上海。他的艺术修养很高，在他的影响下，他家的女眷也精于绘画，尤其擅长刺绣。在当时流行画风的影响下，她们继承宋代刺绣的技巧并在此基础上有所创新——在蓝本上，选择高雅的宋元名画；在技法上，创造出散针、套针、滚针等针法。她们用绘画描摹的技巧来刺绣，使得刺绣作品活灵活现。

顾绣以技法精湛、形式典雅、艺术性极高而闻名。其中以顾名世的二儿媳韩希孟的工艺最为精湛。她所作的山水、人物、花鸟已达到"无不精妙"的程度，连当时著名的画家董其昌都对其称赞有加。如今北京的故宫博物院陈列有她的刺绣作品十余幅，其中的《洗马图》《白鹿图》《松鼠葡萄》《扁豆蜻蜓》皆为精品，这些作品已达到让人分辨不出是绣还是画的意境。

Gu Embroidery

Gu Embroidery refers to the embroidery work by the well-known Gu family in Shanghai in the Ming and Qing dynasties. Gu Mingshi, a first-class scholar from the imperial court examination, was highly cultivated in arts. He lived in Shanghai in his late years. Under his influence, the women in his family were all very good at painting and embroidery. They inherited the embroidery techniques of the Song Dynasty (960-1279) and became very innovative to select famous Song paintings as blueprints

• 顾绣 (图片提供：FOTOE)
Gu Embroidery

for their embroidery works. They invented various stitching techniques. Combined with their expertise in sketching, their embroidery works looked vivid and lifelike.

Gu Embroidery is well-known for its superb techniques, elegant forms and extremely high artistry. The best in the family was Gu Mingshi's second daughter-in-law Han Ximeng. Her embroidery works of landscapes, flowers, birds and portraits had reached the level of perfection and were highly praised by the famous painter Dong Qichang. A dozen of her embroidery works are in the collections of the Palace Museum. Among them, *Painting of Horse Bathing*, *Painting of White Deer*, *Painting of Squirrels and Grapes* and *Painting of Dragonfly on Green Beans* are considered her masterpieces, which are almost impossible for people to distinguish whether they are embroideries or paintings.

Embroidery was a representation of such embroidery craftsmanship.

In addition to embroidery, techniques such as tapestry, appliqué and drawnwork were also applied to fan leaves making the round fan art reach its culmination.

Before the appearance of folding fans, men also used round fans. But traditionally round fans seemed to be exclusively an accessory for women.

- 《瑶宫秋扇图》任熊（清）

图中一位仕女高挽发髻，手执鹦鹉纨扇，低头凝视，姿容秀丽。衣纹线条刚劲、飘洒，时出方折之笔，笔致细腻，设色浓丽，有更多世俗趣味。

Painting of Fairy Palace and Autumn Round Fan by Ren Xiong, Qing Dynasty (1616-1911)

In the picture a beautiful court lady with her hair rolled up high gazes down with a love-bird silk fan in her hand. Her face and her dress are meticulously painted with bright color showing a secular taste.

缂丝

　　缂丝，也称"刻丝"，是一种用特殊工艺编织成的丝织品。制成缂丝需先上好经线，再编织纬线。编织时不贯通全幅，而是把要织的花纹部分留出来，最后用各种染色的丝线编织花纹，这就是通常说的"通经断纬"的编织方法。用这种方法编织出的丝织物，花纹与白底之间存在着一些断痕，就如同用刻刀刻成的，故称"缂丝"（刻丝）。缂丝的立体感很强，在古代是皇家御用的丝织品。因织造过程极其细致，常有"一寸缂丝一寸金"的说法。

Tapestry

The Chinese silk tapestry, also known as "cut silk", is woven by a special weaving technique called "connecting the vertical and cutting the horizontal". Weaving is done first with warps and then wefts with no weft threads carrying through the full width of the fabric leaving an unblended area for the design patterns. The different colored silk threads woven with this technique produce some broken marks between the design patterns and white background in the finished tapestry work. The effect is similar to cutting with a knife; hence the name "cut silk", which creates a three-dimensional impression. Chinese silk tapestries had long been used by the imperial families because of its extremely detailed craftsmanship. There is a saying, "One inch of cut silk worths one inch of gold."

• 明代缂丝衮
Court Clothing with Tapestry of the Ming Dynasty (1368-1644)

• 清代缂丝《麻姑献寿图》
Tapestry Work *Painting of Ma Gu's Birthday Greetings*, Qing Dynasty (1616-1911)

水、人物在扇面中都有体现。到了明代，团扇刺绣明显带有文人的气息，多以宋元时期的绘画作品作为蓝本，采用绘画与刺绣相结合的方法，创作出的作品栩栩如生。当时著名的"顾绣"便是其中的代表。

除了刺绣之外，缂丝、贴花、抽纱等工艺也被运用到扇面上，从而使团扇艺术达到了登峰造极的高度。

虽然在折扇出现之前，男性也使用团扇，但是在传统观念中，团扇似乎仍旧是女性的专属用品。因此无论是诗词还是绘画，"团扇美人"都给人留下了深刻印象。一枚小小的团扇，在女子手中既可以遮面，又可以传情。手持团扇，半掩娇容，一种中国古典女性独特的含

Whether it was in poetry or in paintings, the image of a beautiful woman with a round fan always left people a very deep impression. A classic Chinese woman could use a small round fan to cover her face partially and express her feelings behind the fan in a subtle and refined way.

Round fans' popularity reached another new height in the Qing Dynasty. Manchu women dressed up in Cheongsam with flared sleeves liked to hold an elegant small and round fan in their hands. The bright colorful Cheongsam presented a sharp contrast with the simple and elegant round fan. In the collections of the Palace Museum there is a round fan used by Empress Dowager Cixi. It has a redwood frame and a white fan leaf with a court-style brush painting demonstrating its extravagance.

Fan cases usually have a rectangular

- 《簪花仕女图》周昉（唐）
Painting of Court Ladies with Hairpin Flowers by Zhou Fang, Tang Dynasty (618-907)

蓄蕴藉、矜持娇柔之美呼之欲出。

到了清代，团扇又迎来了一个新高峰。清代满族女性特有的大摆宽袖的旗袍配以精巧雅致的团扇，使旗袍倍增生机。色泽艳丽的旗袍与清秀淡雅的团扇形成鲜明的对比。北京故宫博物院珍藏着一柄当年慈禧太后用过的团扇——红木扇框，白色扇面，工笔彩绘，非常华贵。

扇匣是一个类似于箱子的长方形物体，多为木质，在南方的部分地区也有用竹子的。上好的扇匣，多用名贵的红木、黄梨木、紫檀木打造，并在上面裱上锦缎。

shape and are mostly made of wood. In some areas in the south bamboos are used to make fan cases. High quality fan cases are made from expensive wood such as redwood, scented rosewood and sandalwood mounted with brocade.

- 身着清朝宫廷服饰，手拿团扇的女子
  Woman Dressed in Court Clothing of the Qing Dynasty (1616-1911) Holding a Round Fan

团扇在民歌中的传唱

中国古代的民间诗歌中,以团扇作为吟咏对象,来表达心声的有很多。流传在魏晋时期的《团扇郎歌》就是其中的一首。

《团扇郎歌》的产生,与西晋时期一个名叫谢芳姿的女子有关。谢芳姿是一名婢女,与当时的中书令王珉产生了恋情。后来他们的恋情被谢芳姿的主人发现,主人便狠狠地打了她。谢芳姿善于唱歌,受到鞭打之后,就将心里的委屈编成歌曲唱了出来。因为平时王珉手中总是拿着一把白色的团扇,于是她就吟道:"青青林中竹,可作白团扇。动摇郎玉手,因风托方便。团扇复团扇,持许自遮面。憔悴无复理,羞与郎见面。"意思是说:竹林中青翠的竹子,可以做成白色的团扇。你手中轻摇团扇,让风带去我的思念。团扇啊团扇,我用它遮挡我的容颜,因为思念而变得憔悴的我,羞于与你相见。后来这首诗流传到了民间就变成了《团扇郎歌》。

与《团扇郎歌》相似的还有《答王团扇歌》,这是东晋时期一个名叫桃叶的女子创作的。她与东晋著名的书法家王献之相爱,王献之曾经作《桃叶歌》给她,表达自己对她的爱慕之情。桃叶便作了《答王团扇歌》来回应他。在诗中她写道:"七宝画团扇,粲烂明月光。与郎却暄暑,相忆莫相忘。"意思是说:我在团扇上画上七宝图案,扇子变得光彩夺目。扇子能给你扇风祛暑,你一定要记住我,不能忘啊。诗中她唱出了自己心中对王献之的想念之情,并希望与他白头偕老。

● 《落花独立图》余集(清)
Painting of Falling Flowers and Lonely Woman by Yu Ji, Qing Dynasty (1616-1911)

Round Fans in Folk Songs

Many Chinese folk songs used round fans as the theme to express feelings. *The Round Fan Lover Song* in the Wei and Jin dynasties is an example of these folk songs.

The song came from a love story about a woman named Xie Fangzi in the West Jin Dynasty. Xie was a maid and she fell in love with Wang Min, a scholar official. When Xie's master found out their love affair, he beat her up. Good at singing, Xie sang to the round white fan used by Wang Min to express her grievances: "Green bamboos can be used to make the round white fan; wave your round white fan and let the breeze bring my thoughts to you. I cover my face with the round fan because I miss you so much that I turn thin and pale; I am ashamed to see you with my pallid face." When the song spread among people, it became *the Round Fan Lover Song*.

Another similar song was *the Round Fan Song to Wang* by a woman named Tao Ye in the East Jin Dynasty. She fell in love with Wang Xianzhi, a famous calligrapher in the East Jin Dynasty. Wang wrote a poem *Ode to Tao Ye* to express his feelings for her. In return, Tao Ye wrote *Round Fan Song to Wang*, in which she said, "I painted seven treasure patterns on the round fan to make it dazzle; the fan can give you breeze and keep you away from heat. When you see the fan, you will never forget me." She conveyed her thoughts for Wang and her hope to stay together with him until they die in the song.

> 折扇

　　折扇，古代称"聚头扇"，因其收起时能够将两头聚合而得名。折扇自出现至今在形态上变化不大，主要由扇骨、扇面两大部分组成。扇子合拢后，外边的两个大的扇骨，称"大骨"或"扇柄"，中间众多的小扇骨，称"小骨"或"芯子"。扇芯连扇边的总根数一般称为"档"或"方"，一般较为常见的档数是14、16、18。扇骨最下部汇合的地方，称为"扇头"，扇头是由"扇钉"聚合在一起的。

　　一把普通的成品折扇，需经几十道工序才能制作完成。首先，制作扇骨需经过破料、劈削、造型、蒸煮、烤晒、打磨、油漆、装配。其次，制作扇面则需纸张开料、糊面、折面、通面、沿边。

> Folding Fans

Folding fans were known as "Heads Together Fans" in ancient times because when the fan was folded the two ends came together. The form and style of folding fans had not changed much ever since the beginning. A folding fan consists of two main parts: the leaf and sticks. When the fan is folded, the outermost two sticks are guards and those small ones in the middle are sticks. The total number of sticks commonly seen is 14, 16 and 18. The end of the fan where all sticks come together is called the fan head. The sticks are held together by a movable fan rivet at the fan head.

　　A finished folding fan has to go through dozens of construction steps. Fan sticks have to be roughly shaped, then shaved down to required sizes, carved, dried in the sun, polished, painted and

扇芯
Fan Center

扇面
Fan Leaf

• 折扇的结构
Folding Fan's Construction

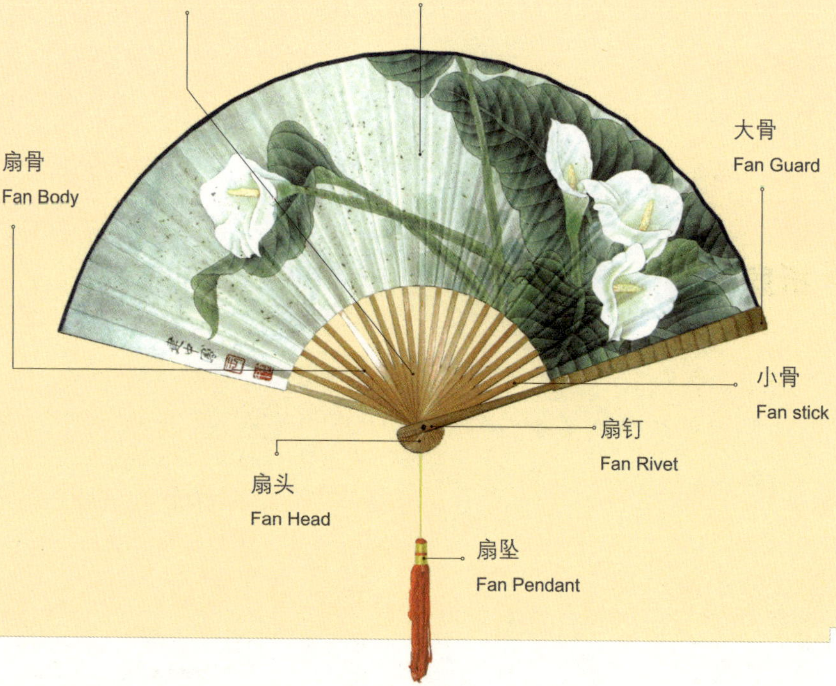

扇骨
Fan Body

大骨
Fan Guard

小骨
Fan stick

扇钉
Fan Rivet

扇头
Fan Head

扇坠
Fan Pendant

折扇制作工艺
Folding Fan Production Process and Techniques

• 制作小扇骨
Make Fan Sticks

• 将小扇骨串联在一起做成扇芯
Connect Fan Sticks Together to Form the Fan Center

- 制作扇子最外面的两个大扇骨

  Make the Two Fan Guards for the Outer Sides of the Fan

- 安装上一边大扇骨

  Install a Fan Guard on One Side of the Fan

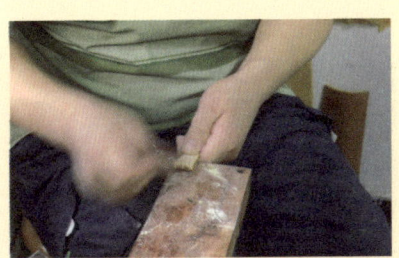

- 在扇骨下部打眼，以安装扇钉

  Drill a Hole on Each Fan Stick for the Fan Rivet

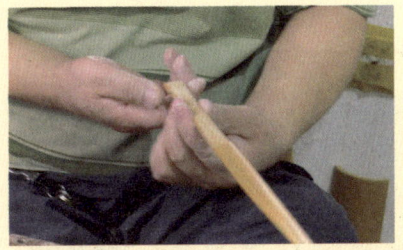

- 安装扇钉

  Install the Fan Rivet

- 制作完成的一把扇骨

  A Finished Fan Body

明代中期以后，随着人们对折扇喜爱程度的日渐高涨，折扇的制作工艺也日益考究起来。在扇骨的材质选择上，以珍稀天然竹质为材料的扇骨最佳，如湘妃竹、梅鹿竹、棕竹、桃丝竹、罗汉竹及玉竹等。木质中的紫檀木、红木、乌木、鸡翅木、檀香木、黄杨木、金丝楠木也是上等的扇骨材质。另外，还有更为名贵的象牙、玳瑁扇骨。

assembled. To make the paper fan leaves, it's necessary to get the paper cut, glued, pleaded, molded and trimmed.

After the mid-Ming Dynasty, the craftsmanship of folding fans became more sophisticated with their increasing popularity. In the selection of raw materials for fan sticks, the best are rare types of bamboos which include mottled bamboo, merlot bamboo, black bamboo, kuma bamboo and makino bamboo. Rare types of wood are also used for making

● 竹子
Bamboo

● 紫檀木
Rosewood

扇骨的制作工艺则有雕刻、镶贴、镶嵌、髹漆、烫花、手绘等多种样式。扇面分有色面和素面。有色面以金面最讲究，有泥金、洒金、屑金、冷金、半冷金；素面分纸面、绢面、发笺等。

fan sticks such as rosewood, redwood, ebony, wenge, sandalwood, boxwood and gold-thread phoebe. The most valuable fan sticks are made of ivory and tortoiseshell.

Fan sticks can be carved, pieced, engraved, enameled, ironed and hand painted. The fan leaves have two kinds: colored and plain. In colored fan leaves gilded ones are the most complicated using a variety of gilding techniques such as "gold mud", "sprinkling gold", "gold scraps", "cold gold", etc. Plain fan leaves include regular paper ones, silk ones and *fajian*, an ancient type of craft paper.

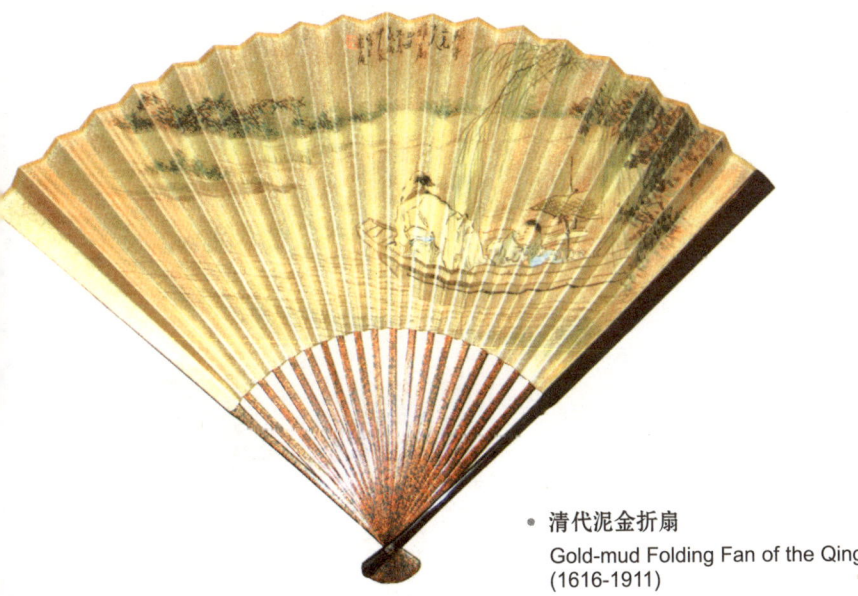

• 清代泥金折扇
Gold-mud Folding Fan of the Qing Dynasty (1616-1911)

泥金、洒金

泥金：是将金箔或金粉与胶混合在一起和成泥状，将它涂饰在白扇面上，成泥金扇面。

洒金：先在扇面上施胶（通常为牛羊骨胶），将金箔洒在扇面上。大如雨滴小如芝麻的细碎金箔密集地洒在扇面上，通称"雨金""细洒金"；如雪花般大片分布在扇面上，称"片金"；如雨般更密集地几乎布满扇面，则称之为"冷金"。一面冷金，一面为素面称为"半冷"。还有将洒金素面互掺成扇面的，称二格金（一素一金）、三格金（一素二金，一金二素）、四格金等。

Gold Mud and Sprinkling Gold Fan Leaves

A gold-mud fan leaf is made from mixing gold foil and gold powder together with glue to make it sticky like mud. Then this mixture of gold mud is applied to the fan leaf surface.

The "sprinkling gold" technique is to first apply glue (most commonly used is cattle and sheep bone glue) to the fan leaf and then sprinkle tiny gold foil chips densely on the fan leaf. This technique is called "gold rain" or "sprinkling fine gold". If the gold foil chips are as big as snowflakes, they are called "gold flakes". If these bigger gold flakes are applied to the fan leaf in an extremely dense fashion, the technique is called "cold gold". If one side of the fan leaf is gilded and the other side is plain, the technique is called "semi cold gold". If the fan leaf has some gilded segments and some plain segments, the technique is called "two gold segments" (meaning one gold one plain), or "three gold segments" (one plain with two gold or one gold with two plain) or "four gold segments", etc.

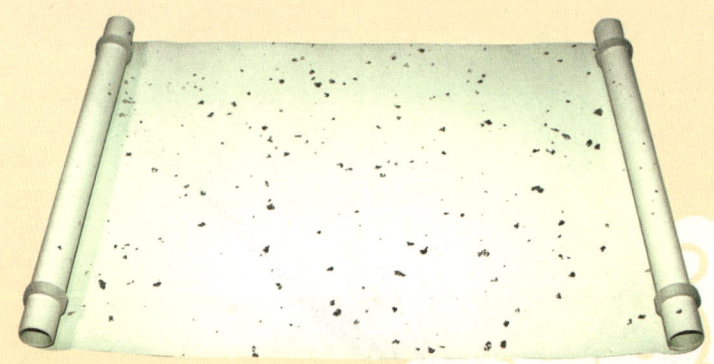

- 清代洒金绿蜡笺纸

Paper Sprinkled with Gold Foil Chips and Green Wax Powder of the Qing Dynasty (1616-1911)

发笺

又称"苔纸",是古代一种纸的名字。由于这种纸的表面有纵横交织的如同婴儿毛发般的丝絮而得名。其制造方法是:先以麻类、树皮为主要原料制浆,在捞纸前于浆内掺入少量水苔作为填料,以此来增加纸张纤维抗拉力的强度;经搅拌均匀后再打槽浇纸,成品的纸面上就呈现出纵横交织的有色纹理(苔丝),故称"苔纸"。

Fajian

Fajian is the name of a type of paper used in ancient times. Its papermaking procedure started with soaking fibers from tree barks and hemps in water to form slurry. Then a small amount of sphagnum moss fiber added for the purpose of strengthening the adhesion of the paper. The slurry was sloshed around in the screen mold to form a thin paper layer. After layers of paper fiber were pressed and dried, sideway laid lines and top-to-bottom chain lines caused by the screen mold appeared on the paper. The lines on the paper looked like baby hair, hence the name *Fajian* (*fa* means hair and *jian* means paper in Chinese). It was also known as the "moss paper".

扇钉被誉为一把扇子的点睛之笔,扇钉的好坏直接关系一把扇子的成败。一般常见的扇钉有牛角钉、铜钉和银钉。铜钉、银钉多见于北方,其材质较硬,常用在尺寸

A fan rivet is considered the finishing touch of a fan, determining whether this fan can function or not. Common rivets are made of ox horns, copper or silver. In the north of China, copper and silver rivets are usually used in large ebony and

• 清代泥金折扇
Gold-mud Folding Fan of the Qing Dynasty (1616-1911)

较大的乌木扇骨和紫檀木扇骨上。牛角钉中有用黑牛角烫出的扇钉，呈圆拱状，乌黑匀圆光亮，俗称"老鼠眼"，多见于清末民国扇骨；有用白牛角烫出的扇钉，钉色浅而透明，中心有一黑点，俗称

rosewood fan sticks due to their hardness. Rivets made from black ox horns have a round shape and a shining black color. They are also known as "mouse eyes" and were mostly used in fan sticks in the late Qing Dynasty. Those that are made from white horns have a light transparent

扇骨、扇头样式图

扇骨的样式：直式方头扇骨、螳螂腿、和尚头、波折式。直式方头扇骨是折扇中最早出现、最简洁大方的样式。

扇头的样式：大圆头（和尚头）、小圆头、平头、尖头（尖根）、方头（方端）、玉兰头、排笏、古方、燕尾、梅花、竹节、鱼尾、鸭头、如意头等。

Styles of Fan Guards and Fan Heads

Fan guard styles: straight guards with a square head, mantis leg, monk head, wavy style. The style of straight guards with a square head is the most common style for folding fans, simple and elegant.

Fan head styles: round head (monk head), small round head, flat head, pointed head, square head, magnolia head, sparrow tail, plum flower, bamboo strips, fish tail, duck head, Ruyi head, etc.

• 扇骨及扇头样式
Different Styles of Fan Guards and Heads

"鸟眼钉"。除了在牛角上烫出圆拱面外,更为讲究的是要在拱面上烫出图案来,如烫成梅花、太极、万字纹以及福、禄、寿、喜等字。

此外,扇坠的好坏也直接影响着一把折扇的整体水平。制作扇坠的材料很广泛,有玉石、楠木、玛瑙、琥珀、象牙、珊瑚、水晶、沉香等,其中以玉石扇坠最为常见。除了这些名贵的材质之外,还有用桃核、杏核、橄榄核雕刻的扇坠,新奇巧妙,也深受人们的喜爱。常见的扇坠图案多为双鱼、蝴蝶等祥瑞之物,也有根据个人的喜好而雕刻的形状。

color with a black dot in the center. They are called "black eye rivets". An ox-horn fan rivet is ironed into an arched surface, more expensive ones usually having patterns such as plum flowers, Taichi signs or Chinese characters of fortune, wealth, longevity and happiness.

The quality of a fan pendant also affects the overall quality of a folding fan. Materials used to make fan pendants are quite extensive, including jade, phoebe, agate, amber, ivory, coral, crystal and aquilaria. Jade pendants are the most commonly seen. Novice pendants carved from walnuts, apricot kernels and olive pits are well-liked by people. Common fan pendant designs include double fish and butterflies, which are considered auspicious. Pendants can also be custom made based on personal tastes.

- 橄榄核雕刻扇坠
  Carved Olive Pit Fan Pendant

● 明代象牙镂雕蟠螭坠
Pierced Ivory *Panchi* Pendant (*Panchi* Is a Mythical Dragon without Horns) of the Ming Dynasty (1368-1644)

● 清代象牙侍女坠
Ivory Pendant Carved with Maid of the Qing Dynasty (1616-1911)

在古代，小小的一个扇坠就像一张表明身份的名片，它彰显着持扇人的品性。据说著名学者章太炎曾经用袁世凯赠送给他的一枚勋章作为扇坠，以此来表示他对袁世凯的不满和蔑视。

折扇一般还要配以扇袋。扇袋又称"扇囊""扇套"，是专为装扇子而缝制的袋子。袋子的上部有一根丝带，可以挂在腰间。扇袋在明、清两代普遍流行，当时的男子一般都会配在腰间悬挂。扇袋的材质一般为丝绸，上面绣有精美的图案，如诗词文字、山水人物、鸟兽

In ancient times, a small pendant was similar to a modern day business card representing the owner's social status and character. It is said that once the famous scholar Zhang Taiyan (1869-1936) used a medal presented to him by Yuan Shikai as his fan pendant to demonstrate his contempt and dissatisfaction against Yuan.

A folding fan is usually matched with a fan bag. The bag is specifically

- 清代贡缎彩绣扇套
  Satin Embroidery Fan Bags of the Qing Dynasty (1616-1911)

- 明代金香囊
  Gold Sachet of the Ming Dynasty (1368-1644)

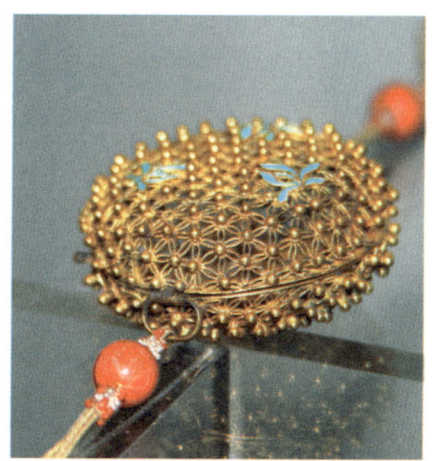

- 金累丝香囊
  香囊是明、清两代的人悬挂在腰间或衣服大襟上的佩饰。
  Gold Thread Sachet
  Sachets were accessories people wore on their clothes in the Ming and Qing dynasties.

草虫、花卉蔬果等。文人一般喜欢梅兰竹菊、高山流水这类雅致的图案，而普通百姓更爱花鸟、如意、八仙这类吉祥喜庆的图案。

杭州是盛产名扇的名城，自古

made in harmony with the fan. The bag has draw strings so that it can be easily tied to the belt. Fan bags were very popular in the Ming and Qing dynasties. Most men at the time had a fan bag on the belt. Fan bags were usually made of silk

以来就有"杭州雅扇"之称。杭州扇以黑纸扇最为著名。这种扇用料讲究，做工精细，美观实用。它的扇骨是采用贵州的棕竹制作而成，扇面用纯桑皮纸做材料，并在上面涂柿漆。经过这样处理的扇面不怕日晒雨淋。曾经有人做过实验，将这种黑纸扇放在水中浸泡十个小时后，从水中取出，不但扇面没有破，而且连颜色也没有改变。故此，杭州黑扇也有"一把扇子半把伞"的美誉。

折扇虽然出现的时间比团扇晚，但是折扇的收藏从明代就开始了。清代折扇的收藏也不乏其人，据说乾隆皇帝就是一位喜欢收藏折扇的名家。他收藏有元明时期的扇子三百多把。近代著名的画家吴湖

with patterns such as poetry, calligraphy, landscapes, portraits, birds, animals, insects, flowers, vegetables and fruits. Literati usually preferred elegant designs of plum flowers, orchids, bamboos, chrysanthemums and landscapes. Common people liked birds, flowers, Ruyi scepter and Eight Immortals representing fortune and happiness.

The city of Hangzhou is famous for its production of fans known as "Elegant Fans of Hangzhou" since ancient times. Beautiful and practical black paper fans are the most renowned with expensive raw materials and sophisticated craftsmanship. The fan sticks are made of black bamboo from Guizhou. The fan leaves are made of pure mulberry paper coated with persimmon lacquer, which makes fans weatherproof. Someone did a test by soaking a black paper fan in the water for over ten hours. When it was taken out, the fan leaf was not damaged and the color did not fade. As a result, Hangzhou black paper fans have a reputation of "one fan can function as an umbrella".

• 杭州黑纸扇 (图片提供：FOTOE)
Black Paper Fan of Hangzhou

- 吴湖帆水墨山水折扇
  Folding Fan with Ink Landscape Painting of Wu Hufan(1894—1968)

帆历经二十年，收藏了清代七十二把状元所题写的扇子。当代著名作家老舍喜欢收藏戏曲演员使用过的扇子，他的家中有一百多把戏曲名家如梅兰芳、程砚秋、荀慧生、尚小云使用过的扇子。

　　折扇的收藏分为扇面的收藏和成扇的收藏。扇面收藏主要是扇面书画的收藏。扇面书画要讲究艺术性，书画要精妙，扇面上的题款也是衡量一幅扇面书画价值的重要标准。

　　成扇的收藏，既要看扇面也要看扇骨。扇面除了讲究艺术性之外，所选用的材质也有优劣之分。扇骨除了材质上的区别之外，还有

Folding fans came out later than round fans. But collecting folding fans started as far back as in the Ming Dynasty. The Qing Dynasty saw no shortage of folding fan collectors. It is said that Emperor Qianlong was a famous collector of folding fans. He had over three hundred folding fans from the Yuan and Ming dynasties in his collection. Wu Hufan (1894-1968), a notable contemporary artist, spent over twenty years collecting seventy-two fans inscribed by those scholars who won the first place in the imperial examinations. The celebrated contemporary writer Lao She (1899-1966) liked to collect fans used by Chinese opera actors and he had over one hundred fans in his collection from well-known Chinese opera masters Mei Lanfang, Cheng Yanqiu, Xun Huisheng and Shang Xiaoyun.

　　Collections of the folding fans are divided into collections of fan leaves and collections of the whole fans. A collection of fan leaves mainly comprises paintings and calligraphies on fan leaves. The inscription on the fan leaf is also a very important criterion to determine the value of the painting or calligraphy on the fan.

　　A collection of whole fans not

- **《兰花图》王素（清）**

此扇面构图取偏势。兰丛置于一侧，墨笔写兰叶，朱砂点兰花，清雅而妩媚。其中一片兰叶长出，将兰丛与题款联系起来，从而使画面呈现稳定之势。

Painting of Orchids by Wang Su, Qing Dynasty (1616-1911)

The composition of the fan leaf consists of two sides with orchids painted on one side and inscriptions on the other. The orchid leaves are painted in black ink while orchid flowers are red color dots. One long orchid leaf extends to the inscription side connecting the orchids with the writing to achieve a balanced image on the fan leaf.

- **《枯木寒鸦图》唐伯虎（明）**

画面中枯树从左下角伸出，横斜于整个画面中央，一块大石突兀于树干之前。光秃的枝头上稀疏散落着几只寒鸦，回首从远处飞来的同伴，这与画面左下角那只孤独伫立的寒鸦形成了鲜明对照，更添画面凄楚之感。

Painting of Dead Woods and Jackdaws by Tang Bohu, Ming Dynasty (1368-1644)

In the painting, a dead tree extends from the lower left corner all the way to the center of the fan leaf with a big stone laid in the front. A few jackdaws sit on the bare dead branches with a few more flying in from afar. The one bird standing alone in the lower left corner and all the other birds in the center form a sharp contrast, which presents a sense of desolation and sadness.

清末吴昌硕桃花折扇
Peach Blossom Folding Fan by Wu Changshuo (1844-1927)

装饰上的区别。一般好的扇骨多包含了雕刻、烫花、髹漆等工艺。

除了收藏扇面、成扇之外,与扇子配套的扇坠、扇袋也深受收藏者的喜爱。

only should have artistic fan leaves, but also high quality materials for fan sticks. In addition, crafting of fan sticks differentiates regular and high quality fan sticks. The latter are usually carved, enameled or with heat-pressed patterns.

Folding fan pendants and bags are also well-liked by collectors.

清代象牙雕松下人物扇柄
Carved Ivory Fan Handle with Figures under Pine Tree of the Qing Dynasty (1616-1911)

清代象牙雕花扇柄
Carved Ivory Fan Handle of Floral Patterns of the Qing Dynasty (1616-1911)

签条本

扇面要经过三四层纸的裱糊才能完成。在裱制过程中，要用纸条将扇面隔出空隙，以备插入扇骨。著名的制扇厂家在添加纸条的同时，还会在扇面两端的第一道折痕处多添加两个纸条，纸条上用红字印上生产厂家的名字以及扇面的规格。一般人们称这两个纸条为"签条本"。这是厂家的一种信誉标志，同时也为收藏者提供了简单的鉴定依据。

Labels of Fan Makers

Paper fan leaf making requires gluing of three or four layers of paper sheets. In the gluing process a piece of paper is added to separate the layers so that fan sticks can be inserted. Prominent fan makers insert two additional pieces of paper as their product labels in the first pleat at both ends of the fan leaf. There are fan specifications and the name of the maker on these labels. The labels represent the reputation of the fan maker and are used by collectors as a simple basis for the fan's appraisal and identification.

• 花鸟折扇
Folding Fan Painted with Flowers and Birds

> 蒲葵扇

蒲葵扇就是人们习惯所说的"蒲扇",因其结实耐用、物美价廉,一直以来都深受普通民众的欢迎。根据史料记载,早在西晋时期,中国的岭南地区就已经开始大量生产蒲葵扇了。

蒲葵扇是用蒲葵树的叶子制

> Chinese Palm Leaf Fans

Livistona fans are commonly known as Chinese palm leaf fans. They are durable, inexpensive and very popular. According to historical records, mass production of these fans started as early as the Western Jin Dynasty (265-317).

Chinese palm leaf fans are made of leaves from Livistona, which is a kind of tall evergreen tree growing in Guangdong, Guangxi, Fujian and Taiwan. Because Livistona leaves look like palm tree leaves, these fans are also called "Chinese Palm Leaf Fans".

There are two types of Chinese palm leaf fans depending on different kinds of palm leaves used: regular fans and glass

● 蒲葵树 (图片提供: FOTOE)
Livistona

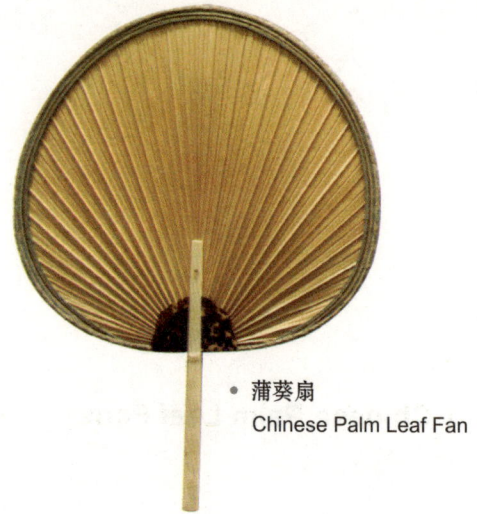

● 蒲葵扇
Chinese Palm Leaf Fan

成的。蒲葵树又称"扇叶葵""葵树",是一种高大的常绿乔木,在中国的广东、广西、福建、台湾等省均有栽培。因为蒲葵的叶子类似芭蕉的叶子,所以蒲扇也被称为"芭蕉扇"。

根据所用蒲葵叶的不同,蒲葵扇分为两大类。一类是普通扇,一类是玻璃扇。普通扇就是把生葵叶割下来晒干,裁剪成扇样,用竹篾夹边,葵柄用藤条缝合,熏焙、漂白即可。因为每次收割蒲葵时,要在其顶端留三个嫩葵叶,看上去像三面旗子,所以也把蒲葵扇叫作"三其(旗)扇"。

玻璃扇是选择蒲葵初发未舒的浅绿嫩叶,经过日晒后,颜色洁白

fans. A regular fan is made of raw palm leaves, which are dried, cut into the fan shape and clamped by bamboo guards. The fan handle is sutured with rattan twigs. Once it is fumigated and bleached, the fan is done. When palm leaves are collected, three tender leaves at the top of each leaf are left untouched, which look like three flags. Therefore, this kind of fan is also called "Three-flag Fan".

Glass fans are made of young palm leaves. When dried, they change to pure white color, which looks like the color of glass. The process of making glass fans is a bit unusual. First young palm leaves are bundled together to prevent penetration of any sunlight so that they can grow into transparent "glass palm" leaves. Then they are cut off from the tree, fumigated in sulfur and washed in water to make glass fans. The most typical "glass fans" are fire painting fans, bamboo shell painting fans and woven fans.

Fire painting fans are one of the four famous types of fans in China. The name came from a specially made "fire pen" used to paint on palm leave fans. It is said that in the Qing Dynasty, Chen Wan, a well-known artist in Xinhui, Guangdong province was the first craftsman to cut and paste paintings and

● 火画扇 (图片提供：FOTOE)
Fire Painting Fan

如同玻璃，因之得名。其加工方法比较特别，要先用禾草将树上还未散开的新生葵叶扎成"葵笔"，使里面不透入阳光，长成特别柔嫩有透明感的"玻璃葵"，然后割下来，经过硫黄熏蒸、水洗加工制成"玻璃扇"。具有代表性的玻璃扇有：火画扇、竹箨（tuò）画扇和织扇。

火画扇是中国四大名扇之一，因用一种特制的"火笔"在葵扇上作画而得名。据说清代同治年间，广东新会的著名画师陈晚，首先将诗画剪贴于玻璃扇上，但一经受潮诗画便会脱落。最后他想出一个办法，将画在扇面上的诗画用香火烙

poetry on glass fans. But the shortcoming of a pasted painting was that when the painting was exposed to moisture it would fall off from the fan. Chen Wan came up with a solution to burn the painting using incense so that the burned painting could be exposed through the fan leaf. This became the original version of fire painting fans. Later people used heated wire instead of incense to iron the painting to the fan leaf. After this procedure, the color of the painting would not fade.

The making of bamboo shell painting fans started with bamboo shells soaked completely and pulps taken out from inside. The outer shell was scraped very thin and dyed into black color. After patterns or designs were carved on the shell, the shell was glued to the bleached palm fan leaf to form a contrast between the black carved shell patterns and the white woven palm fan leaf.

Woven fans were made of dried glass palm leaves which were shredded to very thin strips and bleached. Then the strips were woven into two semi-finished parts. And the final process was to sow the two semi-finished woven parts together to make a finished fan. In the *Historical Records About Xinhui*, Guangdong

焦，以显示出诗画来，这便是最初的火画扇。后来人们不再使用香火而是把铁丝烧红在扇面上烙诗画。用火笔在扇面上烙图案，能长久保持不褪色。

箨是竹笋的表皮。竹箨画扇就是将竹箨浸透，去掉里面的瓤，使用外面的表皮，将其刮薄，染成黑色，然后用刀镂刻出各种图案或花纹，粘贴于漂白的葵织扇上。扇纹与箨纹黑白分明，相映成趣，玲珑雅致。

织扇是先把已晒好的玻璃葵撕成细细的小条，将其漂白，编织成扇坯，然后将两把扇坯交织成一把新扇。据广东《新会乡土志》记载，这种织扇工艺首先是由谭月三首创的，后来新会的扇工都仿制，工艺也日渐精湛。1913年，曾有人将织扇送给梁启超。梁启超见过此扇之后大加赞扬，特书"艺术专精"，从此，织扇声名鹊起。

province, woven fans were first invented by Tan Yuesan and followed by all fan makers in Xinhui. The craftsmanship gradually became more sophisticated. In 1913, Liang Qichao received a woven fan as a gift and wrote "An Artistic Delicateness" to praise its craftsmanship. From then on, woven fans became widely known.

● 织扇 (图片提供：FOTOE)
Woven Fan

梁启超

梁启超（1873—1929），字卓如，号任公，又号饮冰室主人，广东新会人。中国近代著名的政治活动家、启蒙思想家、教育家、史学家和文学家。中国近代维新派领袖，曾经和康有为等人一起倡导维新变法。变法失败后他前往日本，在日期间大量介绍西方社会政治学说，对当时的知识界影响很大。1916年，梁启超赴两广地区参加反对袁世凯的斗争，袁世凯死后，梁启超出任段祺瑞北洋政府财政总长。11月，段祺瑞内阁被迫下台，梁启超也随之辞职，从此退出政坛。1922年起在清华学校讲学，1929年病逝。

Liang Qichao

Liang Qichao (1873-1929) had a courtesy name Zhuoru and pseudonym Rengong, and was known as the Host of Iced Drinks Café. Born in Xinhui, Guangdong province, Liang was a renowned political activist, an enlightened thinker, an educator, a historian and a writer of contemporary Chinese literature. As a representative of the Chinese modern reformists, Liang, together with Kang Youwei, strongly advocated reforms in China. After the reform movement failed, he went to Japan and continued to actively advocate western social political theories, which had a strong influence among Chinese intellectuals. In 1916 Liang went to Guangdong and Guangxi provinces to participate in movements against Yuan Shikai. After Yuan's death, Liang was appointed by Duan Qirui as the Minister of Finance and Inspector General of Salt Affairs. In November the same year Duan was forced to step down and Liang resigned and left politics. In 1922 Liang taught in Tsinghua University and he died in 1929.

● 梁启超像
Portrait of Liang Qichao

神话传说中的芭蕉扇

蒲葵扇，又名芭蕉扇，不仅在日常生活中普遍见到，在中国的神话故事中也不乏手执芭蕉扇的人物形象。最为人熟悉的就是济公和他手里的那把芭蕉扇。

济公在中国是一位妇孺皆知的人物。他本是南宋时期的一名僧人，出家在杭州灵隐寺。但是他生性豪放，好吃肉喝酒，举止癫狂，于是被称为"济癫"。平日里他常手持酒壶，腰插芭蕉扇，行走在市井之中，遇到不平之事能不畏强暴、除暴安良、扶危济困，于是人们称他为"活佛"。

济公手中的芭蕉扇表面上看起来破烂不堪，其实却法力无边。每次济公扶危济困，靠的就是这把破扇子。有一次，济公看到一个年轻人正在欺负一个老婆婆，他便走上前去，加以劝阻。但是那个年轻人不但不听，反而狠狠地瞪了他一眼，叫他不要多管闲事。济公见劝说不管用，就从腰中拿出扇子，轻轻地对着那个年轻人一扇，那个人立刻缩小了一半，再一扇，又缩小一半。眼看着自己越变越小，年轻人赶紧跪在地上求饶。见他已经认错，济公又扇了两下，那人就恢复了正常。现在民间还流传着这样的歇后语：济公的扇子——神通广大。

● 济公铜像
Bronze Statue of Ji Gong

与济公的芭蕉扇一样具有广大神通的，还有古典神话小说《西游记》中铁扇公主的芭蕉扇。铁扇公主的原名叫作"罗刹女"，居住在翠云山芭蕉洞内，因为她有一把神奇的芭蕉扇，所以又被称为"铁扇公主"。她的这把扇子，扇一下可以熄火，扇两下可以生风，扇三下就可以下雨，若是扇到了人，可以把人扇出八万四千里之外。说话唐僧师徒去西天取经的路上，路过火焰山，熊熊大火让人难以靠近，于是孙悟空便去向铁扇公主借芭蕉扇，几经周折，孙悟空成功将山火扑灭，师徒四人又继续上路了。

此外，传说"八仙"中的汉钟离也有一把芭蕉扇，俗称"钟离扇"。八仙过海时，汉钟离把芭蕉扇往海里一扔，然后躺在扇子上就漂向了远方。

Palm Leaf Fans in Chinese Folk Tales

Chinese palm leaf fans are very common in the Chinese daily life. Chinese folk tales also have quite a few characters with palm-leaf fans in their hands. People are most familiar with Ji Gong and his palm-leaf fan.

Ji Gong is a mythic hero widely known in China. He was originally a monastic at the famous Lingyin Temple in Hangzhou in the Southern Song Dynasty (1127-1279). He was called "Ji the Eccentric" due to his wild behavior of meat eating and wine drinking which were not allowed for monks. Every day he showed up in the city streets holding a wine bottle in one hand and a palm-leaf fan in the other. But he had a compassionate nature and was always ready to help out whenever there was a need and whenever he saw injustice.

His palm-leaf fan looked torn, but it had a magic power. Ji Gong relied on his fan to help out those in danger and in a difficult time. Once he saw an elderly lady being bullied by a youngster. He went over to stop the young man, who simply ignored what he said and in turn asked him to go away. Ji Gong then fanned lightly at the youngster, whose body was immediately reduced by half. Ji Gong fanned again and his body became smaller even more. The youngster immediately kneeled on the ground begging for mercy. When he saw him admitting his wrongdoing, Ji Gong waved his fan twice to bring him back to his normal size. Even today there is a Chinese saying that Ji Gong's fan is a powerful magic wand.

Another folk story is about Princess Iron Fan, a fictional character in the classic novel *Journey to the West*. Princess Iron Fan lived in the Palm-leaf Cave of the Green Cloud Mountain. She had a palm leaf fan as powerful as Ji Gong's. When she fanned once, the fire was put out; when she fanned twice, giant whirlwinds were generated; and when she fanned three times, rain poured down. She could fan people as far as eighty-four thousand miles away. In their journey to the west, Monk Tang and his disciples encountered volcanic mountains with extremely hot flames. Sun Wukong, the Monkey King went to Princess Iron Fan to borrow her palm leaf fan. After a few setbacks he was eventually able to obtain the fan and put out the fire so that they could continue their journey.

In the legend about the Eight Immortals crossing the sea, Han Zhongli, one of the Eight Immortals had a palm leaf fan known as Zhongli Fan. He threw this fan on the sea and was able to cross the sea by lying on his floating fan.

> 檀香扇

檀香扇，是中国四大名扇之一，素有"扇中之王"的美誉。檀香扇将折扇的轻便与檀香木的香气合二为一。檀香木，又名"旃檀"，木质坚硬，含有天然的芳香油，香味纯正、淡雅。根据树皮的颜色，有白檀木和紫檀木之分。由檀香木制成的檀香扇具有天然香味，用以扇风，清香四溢。檀香扇保存十多年后，依然幽香阵阵，有"扇在香存"之誉。檀香扇盛暑可以却暑清心，入秋藏之柜中，还有防虫防蛀的功效。

如今的檀香扇小巧玲珑，秀美典雅，多为女性使用。但是在早期，男性也使用檀香扇，因为檀香扇是从折扇演变而来的。早期的檀香扇基本上模仿折扇的规格及式

> Sandalwood Fans

Sandalwood fans are one of the four famous types of fans. It has a prestigious name "the King of Fans". A sandalwood fan combines the lightness of a folding fan with the sandalwood aroma. Sandalwood is a kind of Santalum trees. Sandalwoods are heavy and hard with a fragrant oil scent. There are yellow and white tree barks in sandalwoods. A sandalwood fan, when in use, produces a light aromatic airflow and its fragrance can be retained for decades. Sandalwood fans enjoy the reputation of "as long as the fan is here the fragrance remains". They can be used to get a breeze in the summer heat and are effective in keeping moths away when placed in the closets in autumn.

Today's sandalwood fans are small, delicate, refined and elegant, mostly

● 檀香扇
Sandalwood Fan

样，只是以檀香木篾片局部或全部替代竹骨。20世纪30年代，新颖秀美的日本女式折扇风行东南亚，当时的杭州王星记扇庄从中受到启发，缩小扇子的形制，将扇面改用檀香木连缀，并雕刻以精美的图案。这种扇子一经出现，立刻受到了女性们的喜爱，从此檀香扇由男扇演变为女扇。

　　檀香扇的制作一般经锯片、组装、锼拉、裱面、绘画、上流苏等十多道工序。檀香扇主要的产地有苏州、杭州、广州等。苏州是中国最负盛名的檀香扇产地。苏州的檀香扇式样巧妙，历史悠久，一直以精湛的制扇技艺蜚声中外。苏州檀香扇以"四花"——拉花、烫花、

used by women. But in the early days men also used sandalwood fans because sandalwood fans were evolved from folding fans. The earlier versions of sandalwood fans were made after the shape and style of folding fans. The only difference was that bamboo fan sticks were partially or entirely replaced by sandalwood chips. In the 1930s, novel-looking Japanese folding fans for women became very popular in Southeast Asia. Inspired by its design, a fan maker named Wang Xingzhai in Hangzhou decreased the size of sandalwood fans and used carved sandalwood chips as sticks to make Brisé fans. As soon as they appeared in the market, sandalwood brisé fans won the hearts of women. From then on, sandalwood fans transformed from men's fans to women's.

　　The making of sandalwood fans involves dozens of steps including cutting, assembling, carving, mounting, painting and ribbon-attaching. Suzhou, Hangzhou and Guangzhou are the main producing areas for sandalwood fans, among which Suzhou is the most famous. Sandalwood fans produced in Suzhou have a long history, artful style and high-quality craftsmanship well known in and out of China. Suzhou sandalwood fans

雕花、画花见长。拉花，是在扇骨上用钢丝拉出图案；烫花，是用特殊的电笔在扇骨上画出枯焦色的图画；雕花，是在檀香扇两旁的大骨上雕刻人物、山水、花鸟等；绘花，是在绢面上绘上仕女、山水、花鸟等。

excel in its unique four designs:

Wire-Drilling: To use extremely thin wires to drill holes following the patterns pasted on fan sticks;

Charring: To use a specially made electric pen to produce charred patterns on fan sticks;

Carving: To carve portraits, landscapes, flowers or birds on the two fan guards on either side of the fan;

Painting: To paint women, landscapes, flowers or birds on silk fan leaves.

• 檀香扇烫花工艺
Sandalwood Fan with Charred Patterns

檀香扇的花色品种

檀香扇的花色品种主要有以下六种：

（1）倒肩：绢面比扇篾外露部分来得短，行话称"倒扇"；绢面展开后的造型如桥，因杭州"西泠桥"而得名，称为"西泠"。

（2）格景：绢面由原先统一的圆弧形改为大小不同、不相连续的两块或三块，犹如西湖中游离连绵的湖心亭的景色，故称"两格景"或"三格景"。

（3）全面：又叫"全景"，不用绢面，全用檀香扇篾以彩带或尼龙丝隐在骨内穿成，分层拉出精妙的花纹。

（4）排笳：绢面占全扇的一半，扇肩（扇头到绢面之间的部分）形似两端弯曲的胡笳，故名。

（5）拉烫：拉花与烫花相结合。

（6）镶嵌：在拉花、烫花的图案之中，另外镶嵌牛骨片、牛角片、象牙片或银丝作点缀。

Varieties of Sandalwood Fans

There are mainly six varieties of sandalwood fans:

(1) Inverted edge: The silk fan leaf is shorter than the top edge of the fan sticks. When the fan is open, the fan leaf forms an arch like a bridge. This style is called *Xiling*, which is named after *Xiling* Bridge in Hangzhou.

(2) Grid views: The silk fan leaf is changed from one arch shape into two or three unrelated grids of different sizes. This design looks like a series of small man-made islands in the center of the West Lake in Hangzhou. Therefore, it is called "two-grid view" or "three-grid view".

(3) Panoramic view: The silk fan leaf is replaced by sandalwood fan sticks sowed together with ribbons or nylon threads inside. This design produces multi-level patterns.

(4) Flute: The silk fan leaf only covers half of the fan and the other half called the fan shoulder(between the fan head and the leaf) looks like Hujia, a traditional Chinese flute.

(5) Drilled and charred: A combination of drilled and charred patterns.

(6) Mosaic: In the drilled or charred patterns, pieces of horns, bones or ivory and silver threads are inlaid as decorations for fan sticks.

> 象牙扇

象牙扇有象牙宫扇和象牙折扇之分。它是利用象牙细致的纹理与不易碎的韧性，将其劈成厚薄宽窄均匀的象牙丝，编织成扇面。为增加扇面的立体感，会再用象牙制成

> Ivory Fans

Ivory fans consist of ivory court fans and ivory folding fans. Thanks to its fine striations and unbreakable hardness, ivory can be cut into thin threads of uniform sizes to weave fan leaves. In order to create three-dimensional images, ivory

---

花中四君子——梅兰竹菊

梅花、兰花、竹子、菊花，被中国人称为"花中四君子"。它们是咏物诗和文人画中最常见的题材，其共同特点是，清华其外，淡泊其中，不作媚世之态。它们分别代表的是高傲、幽雅、坚韧、淡泊的性格品质。

Four Noble Gentlemen: Plum Blossom, Orchid, Bamboo and Chrysanthemum

Plum blossoms, orchids, bamboos and chrysanthemums are considered by the Chinese "four Noble Gentlemen" among all plants. They have always been the subjects in poetry and paintings by Chinese literati. Their common characteristics are full of strength, simple, honest and never seeking favor by flattery. They respectively represent nobility, elegance, persistence and simplicity.

- 象牙雕梅、兰、竹、菊团扇
  Round Carved Ivory Fans of Plum Blossom, Orchid, Bamboo and Chrysanthemum

浮雕的花卉、人物、花鸟、昆虫等固定在扇面上，组合成富有吉祥寓意的纹样。

象牙扇多产自广东，是宫廷专用制品。北京故宫博物院藏有数十件各种形状、纹饰的象牙丝宫扇。其中一把以象牙篾丝编缀的雕花团扇，是清代乾隆年间广东官员进献宫廷的礼品。此扇形状如芭蕉叶，扇面用洁白细薄的象牙丝编成。全扇突出了象牙丝细腻润泽的质感，庄重典雅，古色古香。

embossments of figures, birds or insects are fixed on fan leaves to form auspicious patterns.

Most ivory court fans were produced in Guangdong province. There are dozens of ivory court fans of different shapes and designs in the collections of the Palace Museum. One of them is a round fan woven with ivory threads and carved patterns. This round fan was offered as a tribute to Emperor Qianlong of the Qing Dynasty. The fan has a palm-leaf shape and a white fan leaf woven with extremely thin, pure white ivory threads. The fan highlights the elegance and exquisiteness of the classic ivory art.

> 其他扇子

除了以上常见的各类扇子之外，还有一些别具特色的扇子。

麦秸扇

麦秸扇又称"麦秆扇""麦扇"，是在中国广大农村普遍使用的一种扇子。据史料记载，早在隋朝山西省就已经生产麦秸扇。现在麦秸扇主要产于河北、山东、江苏、浙江等地，尤其以浙江浦江的麦秸扇最为著名。

麦秸扇是用紧挨着麦穗的一截麦秆编织而成的，根据编织方法的不同，有团扇、贴扇、扎花扇、串扇、平扇之分。最简易的一种是团扇，先将麦秸编成麦秸辫，再将麦秸辫盘成一个圆形的扇面，最后在扇面中间固定两片剖开的竹片作

> Other Fans

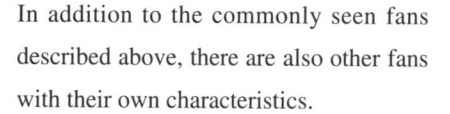

In addition to the commonly seen fans described above, there are also other fans with their own characteristics.

Wheat Straw Fans

Wheat straw fans are used widely in the rural areas of China. According to historical records, Shanxi province started to make wheat straw fans as early as in the Sui Dynasty (581-618). Currently the main production areas of wheat straw fans include Hebei, Shandong, Jiangsu and Zhejian provinces. The most famous wheat straw fans are made in Pujiang, Zhejiang province.

A wheat straw fan is made of the part of a straw right below the wheat ear. Different weaving methods produce different styles of wheat straw fans such as coiled fans, collage fans, mesh fans,

为扇柄，这样一把简易的麦秸扇就做成了。有时为了美观，人们还在上面用彩线绣上一些图案。因为这种扇子制作简便，很多人自己动手就能完成，所以这类麦秸扇最为普遍。串扇是选料最为考究的一种麦秸扇。它要求麦秆粗细要均匀，色泽要洁白，不能有一点儿污渍，也没有折痕。制作时，先将麦秆的一端扎紧，再将麦秆有秩序地加以组合、整理、展平，为使这些麦秆排列有序，往往用绣花细针在麦秆中间串几道线，这就是"串扇"名称的来历。串扇构思巧妙、朴实自然，根根闪亮的麦秆犹如叶脉从柄端向四面辐射而出，尽显其天然的纹理之美。

stringed fans and flat woven fans. Coiled fans are the simplest to make. The wheat straw braids are coiled into a round fan leaf and the handle is made of two cut-open bamboo strips. Sometimes colorful patterns are sowed onto the fan leaf. The method is so simple that many people make the coiled fan themselves. Stringed fans are the most time-consuming. They require white straight and clean wheat straws of uniform size, which are assembled in a specific order and stringed with silk threads. That is where the name "stringed fan" came from. The neatly arranged shining wheat straws on a stringed fan fully display the simple and natural beauty.

Seven-Leaf Fans

In the Han Dynasty (206 B.C.- 220 A.D.), a craftsman called Ding Huan created a fan with seven connected leaves. It was operated by one person and the whole room would get a cooling breeze. However, no details about its making or the theory behind it could be found in the

● 古代竹编吊扇 (图片提供：FOTOE)
Ancient Bamboo Woven Hanging Fan

七轮扇

汉代有一个叫丁缓的人曾经制作了一柄七轮扇。这种扇子由七片相连的扇页构成，一个人操纵，就能让满屋子的人感到凉爽。由于史料记载并不详细，所以并不能具体了解这种扇子的形制与工作原理，但是在中国的部分地区有使用过类似扇子的记录。例如，在清代，徽州婺源地区就曾流行过一种独特的竹编"吊扇"。该"吊扇"共有五片大小相同的竹编扇页，悬挂在房梁上，底部用一根绳子串连。使用时，只要轻轻拉动绳子，扇页就会随之摆动，产生出阵阵凉风。这里的"吊扇"很可能就是根据"七轮扇"改造而来，而最早的"七轮扇"也许可被称为现代电风扇的鼻祖了。

兵器扇

扇子还可以作为兵器使用，灵活自由，可攻可守，收放自如。据《中华古今兵械图考》记载，用于武术的扇子多以铁制折扇为主，长度一般在一尺二寸左右，扇骨为钢或铁制，扇面用麻布和桐油经

historical documents. Similar fans were used in other areas in China. In the Qing Dynasty in Wuyuan, Huizhou area there once appeared a special kind of hanging fans, which had five bamboo woven leaves of the same size. The fan was hung from the ceiling and the leaves were operated by a rope at the bottom of the fan. When the rope was pulled lightly, the leaves started to move and generate breezes for the whole room. This kind of hanging fans might be transformed from the seven-leaf fan, which could be considered the origin of electric fans.

Battle Fans

In ancient China, fans were also used as weapons in attacks and in defense because they were flexible and easy to carry. In the *Study of Weapons in Ancient and Modern China*, fans used in martial arts were mainly iron folding fans. A battle fan was about 1 foot 10 inches long. The fan sticks were made of steel or iron and the fan leaf used linens processed many times in tung oil to make it strong enough to block attacks from hidden weapons. Battle fans were short weapons for close combats when a folded fan could be used as an iron bar and an opened fan could be used as an iron

● 铁扇
Iron Fan

过多次加工制成，坚韧无比，可以阻挡暗器侵袭。由于扇子属于短兵器，所以一般用于近战。合拢就如同一个铁棒，可击打；展开又如同一把钢刀，可砍杀。最常见的是铁扇子，中国古典名著《水浒传》的一百零八将中，就有一个"铁扇子"宋清。在现代的武侠小说中，常常可以见到作为武器使用的扇子。通常使用这种武器的人多是相貌英俊、温文儒雅的武林高手。

槟榔扇

这是用笋箨制作的一种扇子。

knife. The most widely known were steel fans, which originated from a fictional character called Iron Fan Song Qing in the famous Chinese classic *Outlaws of the Marsh*. He was the brother of the main character Song Jiang. Iron fans were commonly found in Chinese martial art novels and used mostly by handsome and well-mannered martial art masters.

Areca Fans

Areca fans are made of bamboo sheaths. When bamboo shoots become ripe, the sheath will fall off. Sheaths are collected, flattened and dried to make fans, which are called areca fans because of the

竹笋成熟之后，外面的笋箨自然脱落，人们将其收集起来，压平晾干做成扇子。因为其颜色与槟榔的颜色相近，所以人们称它为"槟榔扇"。此外，在云南省元江县还有一种用槟榔叶子做成的扇子，当地人也称之为"槟榔扇"。其制作工艺十分简单，先把槟榔叶下面的叶柄砍去，用温水将叶片泡软，之后放入一个凹凸的模型中压干，取出后，安上一个把柄就可以使用了。由于当地气候湿润，所以制作的扇子能保持原始的形态，如果将它拿到气温低的地方，就会变形缩卷，因此当地流传着这样一句俗语："元江槟榔扇，出城三里烂。"

areca brown color. In Yuanjiang County, Yunnan province, the locals call betel-leaf fans areca fans and they are very easy to make. Betel leaves with stalks cut off are soaked in warm water until they become soft. They are pressed into a mold and the fan is done when the leaves are dried. Then a handled is added to the fan. The fan can always maintain its original shape thanks to the humid local climate. When it is brought to a place with a lower temperature, the fan leaf will shrink and curl up. There is a local saying "A Yuanjiang areca fan will go rotten if it is three miles away from the town."

Mayuan fans are black paper folding fans specifically made for Buddhists.

● 折扇
Folding Fan

此外，有专门供佛门使用的马元扇。一般多为黑纸折扇，扇面上写有各种经文，或者是画有弥勒佛、观音、罗汉等佛教人物形象。还有装在靴子里面，专门为旅行准备的靴扇等。

The fan leaves have either scriptures or paintings of Maitreya Buddha, Avalokitesvara or Arhat. There are also fans that can be inserted in boots especially made for travelers.

● 印有佛教人物形象的折扇
Folding Fan Painted with Buddhist Figures

中国古典名著《水浒传》简介

《水浒传》与《西游记》《三国演义》《红楼梦》并列为中国古典四大名著。

《水浒传》的作者是元末明初的施耐庵。该书是一部反映农民起义的长篇小说。主要叙述的是北宋末年朝廷腐败，民不聊生，以宋江为首的108位英雄好汉就汇聚到了梁山之上。他们劫富济贫，替天行道，但是最后还是以失败告终。小说成功地塑造了一系列英雄人物的形象，如宋江、吴用、鲁智深、林冲、戴宗、石秀、武松、李逵、燕青等。

Brief Summary of Chinese Classic *Outlaws of the Marsh*

Outlaws of the Marsh is one of the four great classical novels in Chinese literature.

It was written by Shi Naian of the Ming Dynasty. It is a novel about a Chinese peasant uprising by one hundred and eight outlaws led by Song Jiang against corruptions of the imperial court at the end of the Northern Song Dynasty. They gathered at Mount Liang and acted as Robin Hood on behalf of the heaven to fight for the weak and the poor. But the uprising eventually ended in defeat. The novel successfully created a group of folk heroes including Song Jiang, Wu Yong, Lu Zhishen, Lin Chong, Dai Zong, Shi Xiu, Wu Song, Li Kui and Yan Qing.

- 《水浒传》中的人物——宋江
  Song Jiang, Key Character in *Outlaws of the Marsh*

扇庄、扇幌
Fan Shops and Fan Banners

扇庄

古代称经营扇子的店铺为"扇庄"。因为扇子是季节性很强的产品，一般只在夏季出售，所以卖扇子的同时，很多扇庄还兼营文房四宝等物品，所以扇庄又被称为"纸扇庄"。

历史上著名的扇庄有杭州的王星记扇庄、舒莲记扇庄和张子元扇庄，北京有戴廉增扇庄、三益斋扇庄和福成斋扇庄。其中以王星记扇庄最为有名，被公认为"扇子大王"。王星记扇庄创建于1875年，创始人是王星斋。王星斋是制作高档黑纸扇的名手，他的妻子陈英是制作工艺扇的巧匠。夫妻自设作坊制扇，以选料优、制作精赢得顾客。1934年，"王星记"推出女式檀香扇，因此声名鹊起；后来为适应社会各阶层的需要，又发展了名家书画扇、曲艺扇和舞蹈扇，所经营的扇子有800余种，小的有10厘米的小折扇，大的有100厘米的屏风扇，式样丰富多彩。

Fan Shops

There were fan shops in ancient times. Fans were a seasonal product and usually sold in the summer. Therefore, fan shops also sold stationery on the side, hence the name "Paper and Fan Shops".

Famous fan shops in the Chinese history include Wang Xing Fan Shop, Shu Lian Fan Shop and Zhang Ziyuan Fan Shop in Hangzhou and Dai Lianzeng Fan Shop, San Yizhai Fan Shop and Fu Chengzhai Fan Shop in Beijing. The most famous is Wang Xing Fan Shop known as the "King of Fans". It was founded in 1875 by Wang Xing Fan, who was a master of making high-end black paper fans. His wife Chen Ying was a superb fan craftswoman. The couple started the shop together and won over customers by making high-quality fans. In 1934 they became very famous after putting sandalwood fans specially made for women in the market. Later they developed celebrity painting and calligraphy fans, Chinese opera fans and dancing fans to meet a variety of needs from all walks of life. Their fans had over 800 styles from tiny ten centimeter folding fans to one hundred centimeter screen fans.

扇幌

扇幌是扇庄挂在门前招揽生意用的道具。扇幌的形式尺寸不一。1937年7月，位于北京琉璃厂的"清翰斋"画店，曾制作过一个半径为150厘米、扇面弧线长255厘米、重近8市斤的十骨大扇幌，扇面两侧均为当时著名的戏剧演员剧照图像，色彩鲜艳，造型生动。

Fan Banners

Fan banners of different sizes hung in front of fan shops were an advertising tool to attract customers. In July, 1937 a painting shop called "Qing Han Zhai" in Beijing made a huge 10-stick fan banner, which had a fan leaf of 150-centimeter radius and 255-centimeter long arc. It weighted 4 kilograms. Well-known Chinese opera actor portraits were painted on each side of the fan banner with bright colors producing a lifelike effect.

• 悬挂的扇幌
Hanging Fan Banner

扇之雅
Elegance of Fans

　　当扇子的实用功能逐渐减弱，审美功能逐渐增强之后，扇子与文学艺术的结合就是一种必然。于是，人们在诗词歌赋中看到了文人对扇子的吟咏；在方寸之间的扇面上看到了五彩斑斓的世界；戏曲演员借由一把扇子将人物刻画得淋漓尽致；舞蹈演员在扇子的映衬下翩翩起舞。而民间用扇的习俗，更丰富着中国人的文化，让人们的生活更精彩。

It is inevitable that fans eventually became an integral part of Chinese literature and art as its utility gradually diminished and its artistry was increased. People enjoy poems and proses about fans while looking at a colorful world on fan leaves. Fans are used in folk dances and Chinese operas to vividly portray characters. Fan traditions also make the Chinese culture and art more interesting.

> 扇子与书法绘画

将扇子与传统书画艺术相结合，是中国文人的一大创举。舞文弄墨本是文人所擅长的，他们借扇面的方寸之地施展无限的才华，从而将扇子的实用功能与书画的观赏功能巧妙地结合在一起，实在是中

• 京剧脸谱扇面
Fan Leaf with Paintings of Peking Opera Masks

> Fans with Calligraphies and Paintings

The integration of fans with calligraphies and paintings was a great invention of Chinese literati, whose nature was to write and paint. They demonstrated their unlimited literary talent in a small surface of a fan leaf and skillfully combined the utility of a fan with aesthetics of calligraphy and painting. What a splendor of Chinese ancient fan culture!

Wei and Jin dynasties first saw the appearance of poetry and paintings on fans, which were mainly small decorations since people paid more attention to the utility of fans. According to historical records, Yang Xiu in the Three Kingdoms Period (220-280) was the first person to paint on fans. In the *History of Famous Paintings across Dynasties* by Zhang

国古代扇文化的精彩之笔。

　　在扇子上题诗作画开始于魏晋时期，当时书画还只是作为一种点缀，人们更加注重的仍是扇子的实用功能。有史料记载的第一个在扇面上绘画的人是三国时代的杨修。据唐代张彦元《历代名画记》中记载：杨修曾为曹操画扇面，一不小心掉了一个墨点在扇面上，机智的杨修就顺势将墨点画成了一只苍蝇。当曹操取过扇子观看时，还以为是真的苍蝇，竟然用手去拍打。这就是历史上著名的"误点成蝇"的故事。

　　据说第一个在扇面上题字的人是晋代大书法家王羲之。根据《晋书·王羲之传》记载：一次，王羲之遇见一位面色凝重的卖扇的老妇人，

Yanyuan of the Tang Dynasty (618-907), Yang Xiu accidentally dropped a little black ink on the fan leaf and cleverly made it into a fly when he was painting a fan for Cao Cao. When Cao got the fan, he slapped on it thinking it was a real fly. This became the famous story of "making a fly out of an accidental ink drop" in the history.

It is said that Wang Xizhi, the master of Chinese calligraphy of the Jin Dynasty was the first one to inscribe on a fan. In the *History of Jin Dynasty—Biography of Wang Xizhi*, Wang once saw a somber looking elderly lady selling fans. When asked why she looked sad, she said that she was not able to sell them. So he inscribed on every fan she had and asked her to tell everybody the inscriptions were from Wang Xizhi. Sure enough

• 浙江绍兴题扇桥
Bridge of Fan Inscriptions in Shaoxing, Zhejiang Province

问及缘由才知道原来是因为扇子卖不出去。于是他便给每把扇子都题了字，并告诉她要说这是王羲之的字。老妇人照他说的去卖，果然人人都抢着买。现在浙江绍兴有一个名为"题扇桥"的地方，相传就是当年王羲之为老人题字的地方。

扇面书画真正成为一种绘画形式是在唐、宋时期，这与团扇的盛行密切相关。唐代，团扇书画开始逐渐流行，到了宋代，已经形成了独立的扇面绘画艺术。这时的扇子已经完全从实用的功能中脱离出来，成为绘画的一种载体。团扇精美的形制，为绘画作品平添了一份自然清新之趣。

宋代的统治者喜好丹青，不但成立画院，培养专门的画师，而且还带头创作扇面。宋徽宗尤其喜欢画团扇，曾经先后在一百幅扇面上泼墨作画。他创作的《枇杷山鸟图》最能体现出其绘画风格。圆形绢素上画一棵枇杷树，树上一只小鸟想要啄食枇杷，一只蝴蝶悄然飞过。绘画的笔法简朴，不尚铅华，自然之趣，跃然纸上。他的草书纨扇作品"掠水燕翎寒自转，堕泥花片湿相重"，线条细瘦刚劲，同其

people rushed to buy her fans. Tody there is a place in Shaoxing, Zhejian province named after this story as the "Bridge of Fan Inscriptions".

Popularity of round fans helped to make paintings and calligraphies on fans a form of fine art in the Tang and Song dynasties. As a result, paintings and calligraphies on round fans spread widely in the Tang Dynasty and became an independent school of fan arts by the Song Dynasty. Since then fans grew out of its practical use into a painting art form and the shape of round fans added a natural flavor to fan paintings.

The imperial court of the Song Dynasty was particularly fond of paintings. Painting schools were established to train professional painters. Some of them even did fan paintings themselves. Emperor Huizong of the Song Dynasty had a special affection on round fan paintings and he personally painted over one hundred fan leaves. His round silk fan painting *A Bird in Loquats* demonstrated his typical style, which vividly shows a loquat tree with a little bird pecking at the fruit and a butterfly flying by. His silk fan calligraphy of a verse ("The swallow's feather touches the cold water dropping moist dirt on the flowers") in an

- 《枇杷山鸟图》赵佶（宋）
  Painting of A Bird in Loquats Zhao Ji, Song Dynasty (960-1279)

- 宋徽宗赵佶草书纨扇书法
  Silk Fan Calligraphy in Unrestricted Cursive Script by Zhao Ji, Emperor Huizong of the Song Dynasty

"瘦金体"楷书一脉相承，字迹爽快洒脱，笔势圆润流畅，打破了楷书那种匀称整齐的单字排列的组合方式，从而越发显得活泼。

宋代的扇面绘画题材多为花鸟，山水、人物次之。因为团扇扇面尺寸有限，不宜大肆铺张，所以团扇画面多清新雅致，更多是体现"画意"，即通过画中的景物，使人联想到画外的景致。南宋山水画家马远、夏圭还因此开创了"边角"构图的绘画方式，采用"以小见大"的艺术手法，以局部表现整体，创造出不同凡响的艺术效果，二人分别被人称为"马一角"和

unrestricted cursive script had a slender, firm characteristic similar to his *Shoujin Shu* script, both being free, smooth, and lustrous totally breaking away from rigidly arranged characters written in the regular script.

The Song Dynasty fan paintings focus more on flowers, birds, landscapes and less on figure subjects. Because a fan leaf had a limited space, the painting was mostly clean and simple expressing a conception which would lead the viewer's mind into the landscapes outside of the painting. Ma Yuan and Xia Gui, two landscape painting artists of the Southern Song Dynasty developed a style of "corner" compositions, which produced

"夏半边"。例如,马远的《远山柳岸图》,画面中近景是一座竹桥横斜在水面上,堤岸上是两株枯柳,远处有一带远山隐约可见,此外便没有更多的描绘,但其意境却令人回味无穷。这充分体现了画家删繁就简、爽利峭劲的风格和营造诗意气氛的才能。

北京故宫博物院里收藏了不少宋代团扇书画作品,但大部分没有作者名款,这也是宋代书画团扇的习惯。因为许多团扇书画作品都是画家兴之所至、临时创作的,并不是要以此扬名立世,所以一般都没有落款。此外,因为团扇当时多为女性在室内使用,也不便在上面留名。

团扇既是绘画的载体,也是绘

an artistic effect of "seeing big from small" or showing the totality through one part of it. They were called "Ma the Corner" and "Xia the Half". For example, Ma Yuan's painting *Remote Mountains with Willow on the Riverbank* depicts in close range a bamboo bridge over the water with two dying willow trees on the riverbank and some mountains barely visible in the distance. The picture doesn't have much on itself leaving the rest to the viewer's imagination, which demonstrates the artist's capability to create poetic scenery with a simplistic style.

There are many round fan paintings and calligraphies of the Song Dynasty in the collections of the Palace Museum. But most do not have the artist's name. This was a custom for round fan paintings and calligraphies of the Song Dynasty because most of them were done

- 《远山柳岸图》马远(宋)
Painting of Remote Mountains with Willow on the Riverbank by Ma Yuan, Song Dynasty (960-1279)

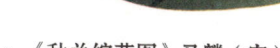

- 《妆靓仕女图》苏汉臣（宋）

图画中一位正在梳妆打扮的仕女，神情娴静而略带忧伤。其面部形象通过镜面表现出来，又以零落的桃花、几竿新竹以及水仙衬托出人物的心境。此图的构图以及人物特征都体现了南宋特色——画面清丽，用色柔美，敷色鲜润。

Painting of Lady in Makeup by Su Hanchen, Song Dynasty (960-1279)

The lady in the painting is applying makeup on her face reflected via the mirror, demure with a little sadness. The background has a few peach blossoms, bamboo and daffodils to serve the character's mood. The painting's composition and the portrait of the character fully demonstrate the soft-color artistic feature of the Southern Song Dynasty.

- 《秋兰绽蕊图》马麟（宋）

画面绘秋兰数茎，兰叶修长劲挺，兰花吐蕊，清丽雅逸。

Painting of Autumn Orchids in Full Bloom by Ma Lin, Song Dynasty (960-1279)

The artist painted several beautiful blossoming orchid flowers accompanied by elegant long leaves.

画的对象。由于团扇本身就具有精巧雅致的特点，加上女性对它的青睐，因此而形成的"团扇美人"的形象，自然成为画家关注的焦点。唐代宫廷画家周昉作有《挥扇仕女图》，画面中的仕女体态丰满，衣着华丽，有的悠然挥扇，有的倚

spontaneously with no intention to make them famous. Therefore, no name was signed on the work. In addition, most round fans were used by women inside of their homes and it was not appropriate for male artists to put their names on the fans.

　　Round fans were a carrier and also

桐沉思，有的忧怨对语，有的闲散梳妆。画家通过对她们日常生活片段的描绘，表现出宫中女子百无聊赖、寂寞空虚的情绪。明代著名画家唐伯虎有《秋风纨扇图》。画中女子手持团扇，立于庭院之中，裙

an object of paintings. An exquisitely made round fan was always a favorite of women. The image of a beautiful woman with a silk fan naturally caught the attention of artists. In the *Painting of Court Ladies with Fans* by Zhou

绢本设色

绢本是指画在绢上的图画。设色是与水墨画区分的画法。因在传统国画中，很多只用水墨，用了颜色的就叫"设色"。简单讲，"绢本设色"就是在绢上画带彩色的画。

Silk Fan Painting and Coloring

Chinese traditional paintings are black ink paintings. Silk fan paintings are basically Chinese traditional paintings with colors.

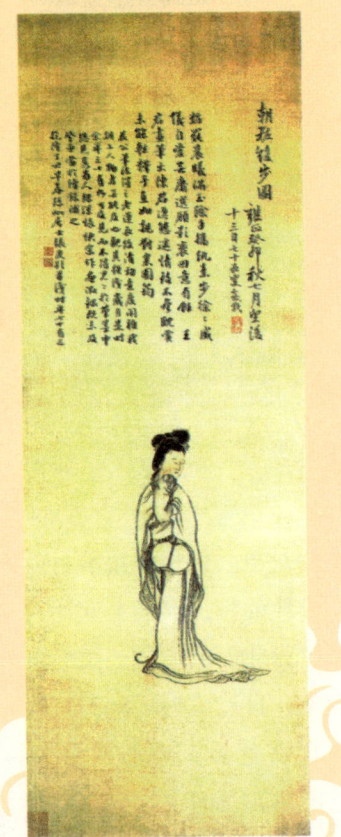

- 《朝妆缓步图》王树毅（清）
  Painting of Strolling in Morning Dress by Wang Shugu, Qing Dynasty (1616-1911)

Fang, an imperial court artist of the Tang Dynasty, some women wave their fans casually; some lean on a tree in deep thoughts; some talk to each other anxiously, and some refresh their makeup idly. They all have a sensual body in gorgeous fashionable dresses. The painting demonstrates their boringness and loneliness through portrayal of their daily life. In the *Painting of Silk Fans in Autumn Wind* by Tang Bohu, a famous artist of the Ming Dynasty, the lady in the painting holding a round fan looks into the distance full of sadness and bitterness

- 《秋风纨扇图》唐伯虎（明）
Painting of Silk Fan in Autumn Wind by Tang Bohu, Ming Dynasty (1368-1644)

- 《挥扇仕女图》周昉（唐）
Painting of Court Ladies with Fans by Zhou Fang, Tang Dynasty (618-907)

角在秋风中飘动。她眺望着远方，眉宇间充满了无限的幽怨和怅惘。画面一角有几株稀疏的细竹，更增添了萧瑟之感。

明代中期折扇书画逐渐流行起来，它突破了传统的绘画和书法模式，在艺术风格、表现手法以及格局设置上都与传统的卷轴画不同。由于扇面的形状呈半圆弧形，其构图也有变化，既要考虑画面景致的视觉平衡，又要使画面随着扇子的形状而改变。故此，明代大画家祝允明曾经形象地把在扇面上作画，比作美女在瓦砾上跳舞，形容画扇面之难。而且折扇扇面质地坚韧光滑，墨汁不容易吸收，稍不留神就会污漫。此外，在金色或黑色扇面上作画写字时，还要注意色彩的配置，与底色不能相犯，因此当时有

in her eyes. She stands in a courtyard with a few scattered bamboos and her dress flutters in the autumn wind. The painting successfully shows a gloomy and somber mood.

In the mid-Ming Dynasty, folding fan paintings and calligraphies gradually became popular having broken through traditional applications of these art forms. The artistic style, techniques of expressions and design patterns were all different from those of the traditional scroll paintings. Because the fan had a semicircular arch, the composition had to be changed in order to maintain the visual balance of the picture changes following the fan's shape. Zhu Yunming, a master painter of the Ming Dynasty compared difficulties of fan painting to dancing on debris. It was very hard for the hard glossy fan leaf to absorb Chinese ink and

• 《竹石图》顾麟士（清）
Painting of Bamboos and Stones by Gu Linshi, Qing Dynasty (1616-1911)

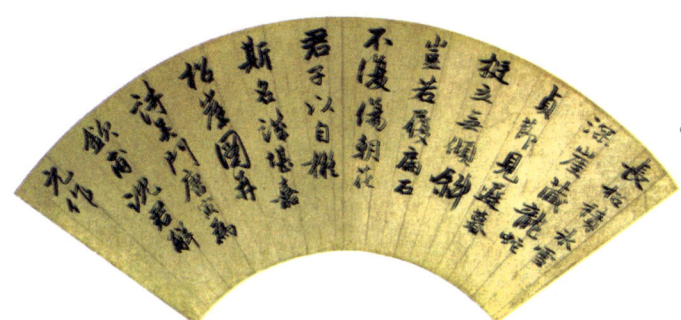

• 明代唐伯虎行书扇面
Calligraphy Fan Leaf by Tang Bohu, Ming Dynasty (1368-1644)

"扇面一尺当二尺，泥金再加倍"的说法。

明代画家沈周、仇英、唐伯虎、文徵明等人都有扇面书画作品传世。唐伯虎的《雨竹图》扇面画，绘雨竹数株，浓淡有致，竹叶披纷下垂，作雨后沾水沉重状。用笔洒脱，寓意深邃。

在明代扇面书画的基础上，清

it was easy to get the fan leaf smeared. In addition, when painting and doing calligraphy on a golden or black fan leaf, the artist had to pay attention to the color configuration to keep it in harmony with the background color. There was a saying at the time that a one-foot long fan leaf had to be treated as if it was two-foot long or more if it was glued with gold foil chips.

• 《雨竹图》唐伯虎（明）
明清时期流行两人甚至多人联合创作扇面书画。这幅扇面就是由唐伯虎绘画，唐伯虎、文徵明、祝允明三人题写诗文。

Painting of Bamboo in the Rain by Tang Bohu, Ming Dynasty (1368-1644)
It was a popular practice to work on a fan painting and calligraphy collaboratively with two or three people. This fan leaf was painted by Tang Bohu with calligraphies from Tang Bohu, Wen Zhengming and Zhu Yungming.

代又有了新的发展。这一时期名家辈出，朱耷、石涛、郑板桥等人都在扇面艺术史上留下了辉煌的一页。

The Ming Dynasty painters including Shen Zhou, Qiu Ying, Tang Bohu and Wen Zhengming all produced renowned fan paintings and calligraphies that were handed down for generations. *Painting of Bamboo in the Rain* is one of the most famous fan paintings of Tang Bohu depicting beautiful scenery of bamboos after the rain.

The Qing Dynasty saw new development in fan leaf paintings and calligraphies. Famous artists such as Zhu Da, Shi Tao and Zheng Banqiao all contributed greatly to the history of fan leaf art.

- **金陵八家扇面三张**

  "金陵八家"是指明末清初的八位画家——龚贤、樊圻、高岑、邹喆、吴宏、叶欣、胡慥和谢荪。他们隐居在南京，以书画为生。他们绘画的题材多取自南京、江淮一带的实景，因而形成了一个画派。

  Three Fan Leaves by Eight Well-known Artists of Nanking

  In the late Ming Dynasty and early Qing Dynasty, there were eight well-known painters: Gong Xian, Fan Qi, Gao Cen, Zou Zhe, Wu Hong, Ye Xin, Hu Zao and Xie Sun. They all lived seclusively in Nanking and made a living on paintings and calligraphies. Most of their works were landscape paintings on areas around Nanking and thus became a school of their own.

钤印

钤印（qián yìn）指书画完成之后的盖章落款，是将刻有作者的名、号的印章印在作品的一角。钤印是很有讲究的。一枚符合画面章法布局和风格特点的印章，会对书画作品起到画龙点睛之奇效。反之则会破坏整个画面布局的协调性，从而降低书画作品的整体质量。

Seal Inscriptions

When a painting or calligraphy is finished, the author stamps the work with a seal carved with his name in a corner of the painting. Seal inscriptions are very particular and can influence the overall quality of the work. If the work has a well-designed seal inscription that matches the style and composition of the painting or calligraphy, it will bring a magic finishing touch to the work. Vice versa it will damage the harmony of the picture and thus lower the quality and the value of the work.

- 《青莲草阁图》石涛（清）
  Painting of Green Lotus Pavilion by Shi Tao, Qing Dynasty (1616-1911)

近现代画家任伯年、齐白石、张大千、徐悲鸿、林风眠、刘海粟、叶浅予等人都有精巧的扇画作品。齐白石喜在泥金纸扇上作画，所画白茶花妍丽动人，蚂蚁和蜜蜂也是精细无比。他的扇面画多为大写意，但其上的鱼虫、花鸟、蔬果无不精致形象，栩栩如生。

Contemporary artists such as Ren Bonian, Qi Baishi, Zhang Daqian, Xu Beihong, Lin Fengmian, Liu Haisu and Ye Qianyu all had exquisite works of fan paintings or calligraphies. Qi Baishi liked to paint on gilded paper fans. His fan paintings of white camellia, ants and bees are exceptionally detailed and refined. His regular paintings are mostly impressionistic, but in his fan leaf paintings of fish, insects, birds, bees, flowers and vegetables are all very meticulous and lifelike.

- 《墨虾图》齐白石（近代）
  Painting of Black Ink Shrimps by Qi Baishi, Modern

- 《重山览清流图》张大千（近代）
  Painting of Hilly Mountains over Clear Streams by Zhang Daqian, Modern

唐伯虎画扇的故事
Stories of Tang Bohu's Fan Paintings

　　唐伯虎是明朝著名的画家，他生性洒脱，机智幽默，至今在民间还流传着许多关于他画扇的故事。

Tang Bohu was a famous painter in the Ming Dynasty. He was intelligent and humorous. There are many folk tales about his fan paintings to the present day.

唐伯虎瓜洲画扇

　　有一次，唐伯虎坐船去瓜洲游玩，看到船老板有一把白纸扇子，唐伯虎说："老板，你这把白纸扇子上面要是有一点儿画就更好了。"船老板看唐伯虎是个读书人，就对他说："那就麻烦你在上面画一画吧。"唐伯虎接过扇子，顺手就画了七只麻雀。船老板一看，很不快意，嘴里就说出来了："你不会画就不要画，麻雀连个眼睛都没有。你看，一把好好的白纸扇子都给你糟蹋了！"唐伯虎说："你既然不喜欢，那我替你拿掉好了。"说着，他用笔在一只麻雀的眼睛上一点，麻雀立即变成活的，飞走了。唐伯虎一连点了六只麻雀，

● 唐伯虎画像
Portrait of Tang Bohu

六只麻雀都飞走了，船老板都看呆了，等他喊停的时候，扇面上就只剩下一只麻雀了。船老板又急忙央求唐伯虎再画几只，唐伯虎说："我的笔只能画一次，画第二次就不灵了。"

Tang Bohu Painted a Fan in Guazhou

One day, Tang Bohu was on a boat to Guazhou and saw the boat owner carrying a white paper fan. So he said to him, "It would be better to have something painted on your white paper fan." The owner saw that Tang looked like a scholar, so he agreed and asked Tang, "Would you mind painting something on it?" Tang painted seven sparrows on the fan. The boat owner was not

- 《牡丹图》唐伯虎（明）
Painting of Peony by Tang Bohu, Ming Dynasty (1368-1644)

very happy and he complained, "If you don't know how to paint, just say it. None of the seven sparrows you painted has eyes. The whole fan is ruined by your painting." Tang said, "If you don't like them, I'll take them out for you." So he used his brush to drop a dot on a sparrow, which immediately became live and flew away. He added dots on each of the six sparrows and they all flew away. The boat owner was stunned and when he screamed to Tang trying to stop him, only one sparrow was left on the fan. The boat owner begged Tang to paint a few more, but Tang said, "My brush can only paint once. It won't create any magic the second time."

唐伯虎画骆驼

有一次，有人来找唐伯虎画扇面，要求他在一个扇面上画出一百只骆驼来。这明显就是在刁难人，但是唐伯虎一点儿也不在意。他先画了一片沙漠，之后又在沙

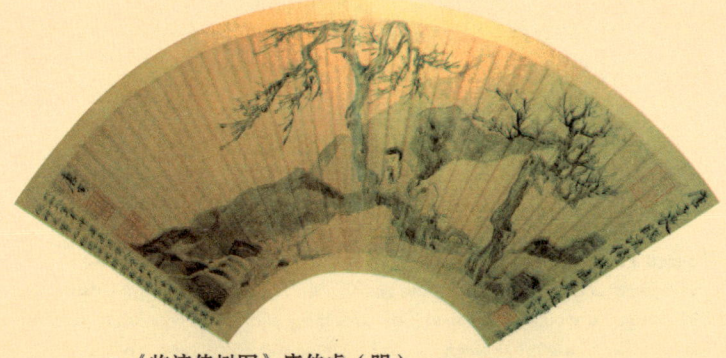

- 《临流倚树图》唐伯虎（明）
Painting of By the River Leaning against the Tvee by Tang Bohu, Ming Dynasty (1368-1644)

漠中画了一座大山，眼看整个扇面已经用去一大半儿，还没见一只骆驼，来人不免有些着急，只见唐伯虎不紧不慢地在山的左边画了一只骆驼的前半身，在山的右边画了骆驼的后半身，之后又在画旁题了一首诗："百只骆驼绕山走，九十八只在山后。尾驼露尾不见头，头驼露头出山沟。"那人一看，哑口无言，只能灰溜溜地走了。

Tang Bohu's Camel Painting
Once a man asked Tang Bohu to paint one hundred camels on a fan leaf. Obviously this man was trying to make things difficult for Tang. But Tang did not care at all. He first painted a desert and then a big mountain on the desert leaving almost no space for any camel. When the man was getting more and more anxious, Tang painted the front half of a camel on the left side of the mountain and the other half on the right side of the mountain. In addition, he added a poem on the painting, "One hundred camels walk around the mountain; ninety-eight of them are behind the mountain with the first one showing his head and the last one showing his tail." The man was speechless.

• 《后溪图》唐伯虎（明）
Painting of Back Creek by Tang Bohu, Ming Dynasty (1368-1644)

> 扇子与诗词小说

中国是一个诗的国度，感情丰富的中国人喜欢将自己的感情投注到一些具体的物象上面。扇子，这一常见而又精巧别致的事物，自然成为诗人们吟咏的对象。

《团扇诗》（又名《怨歌行》），是中国现存最早的咏扇诗，作者是西汉时代的班婕妤。"婕妤"并不是作者的名字，而是汉代后宫嫔妃的一个封号。班婕妤青春妙龄时被汉成帝选入宫中，因为才华出众，不久便被封为"婕妤"。但是注重美色的汉成帝在新妃子进宫之后，便冷落了班婕妤。失宠后的她住在长信宫，深秋的夜晚，独自一人想着昔日的恩宠与今日的疏远，不禁满怀感伤。高墙深

> Fans in Poetry and Novels

China is a country of poetry and the Chinese like to express their feelings and emotions through physical objects. Fans are common, but also can be exquisite and elegant, which naturally become a chanting object by poets.

Ode of a Round Fan, also known as *Song of Resentment* is the earliest fan poem recorded in China. It was written by Ban Jieyu. Jieyu was not the name of the author, but one of the titles given to palace concubines. Ban was selected by Emperor Cheng of the Han Dynasty as a palace concubine when she was young. She was given the title Jieyu because of her talent and intelligence. But as new concubines came into the palace, Emperor Cheng soon forgot all about her, leaving Ban alone in the Changxin Palace.

院，没人可以倾诉，只能将满腔的愁苦化作诗行，于是便有了这首流传千古的《团扇诗》："新裂齐纨素，鲜洁如霜雪。裁为合欢扇，团团似明月。出入君怀袖，动摇微风发。常恐秋节至，凉飙夺炎热。弃捐箧笥中，恩情中道绝。"这首诗

Thinking about the time when she was the Emperor's favorite and her current estrangement, Ban turned her sadness into a poem, which is the *Ode of a Round Fan* known for generations till the present day. The poem goes, "The woven brocade is white and pure like snow; make a round fan with it and the fan leaf shapes like a full moon; carry it with you and fan breezes everywhere; but when autumn comes, cold wind drives heat away and you throw the fan into a box; and the deep feeling is discontinued." In the poem, Ban compared herself to a round fan expressing the bitterness of a palace concubine deserted by the emperor.

In the Wei and Jin dynasties, literary

- 《千秋绝艳图》之挥扇的仕女【局部】佚名（明）

  此卷在6米多长的画面上，绘写了近70位古代仕女形象，包括从秦到明各个朝代中比较著名、见诸史实或传说并在社会或历史上有一定影响的女性，称作《千秋绝艳图》。画中人物都手持或配有最能代表和体现她们身份的配物。

  A Lady Holding a Fan from *Painting of Unique Women in History* (Partial) by Anonymous, Ming Dynasty (1368-1644)

  This is a scroll painting of six meters long portraying about seventy women from the Qin Dynasty to the Ming Dynasty. They are all legendary women who had certain influence in the Chinese history. In the painting each of them wears or holds an accessory that matches their social status.

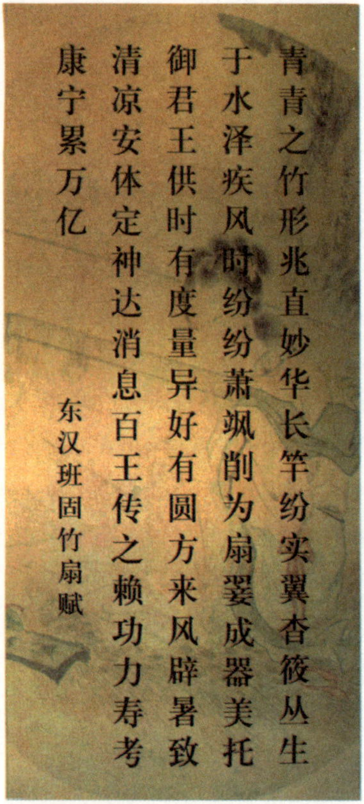

《竹扇赋》班固（东汉）
On Bamboo Fan by Ban Gu, Eastern Han Dynasty (25 – 220)

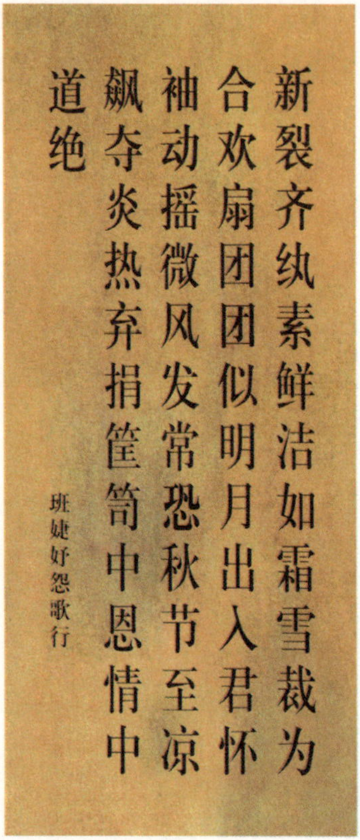

青青之竹形兆直，妙华长竿纷实翼杳筱丛生于水泽。疾风时纷纷萧飒削为扇翣成器美。托御君王供时有度，量异好有圆方来风辟暑致清凉。安体定神达消息，百王传之赖功力，寿考康宁累万亿

东汉班固竹扇赋

《团扇诗》班婕妤（西汉）
Ode of a Round Fan by Ban Jieyu, Western Han Dynasty (206 B.C – 25 A.D.)

新裂齐纨素，鲜洁如霜雪。裁为合欢扇，团团似明月。出入君怀袖，动摇微风发。常恐秋节至，凉飙夺炎热。弃捐箧笥中，恩情中道绝

班婕妤怨歌行

的意思是说：刚织好的一块锦缎，颜色洁白如霜雪。将它做成一把团扇，圆圆的扇面就像一轮满月。你随身携带着它，团扇一摇，阵阵微风拂过。当秋天到来，阵阵凉风驱走了炎热，你也将团扇丢弃在了箱子当中，曾经的恩情也就从此断绝

works about fans came out one after another. Lu Ji, a scholar in the Western Jin Dynasty described in details the beauty of feather fans in his article. As a result, feather fans gained great prominence were greatly promoted. Ban Gu, a writer in the Eastern Jin Dynasty wrote in his work about the bamboo fan

了。在诗中她用"团扇"自喻,写尽了嫔妃受帝王玩弄最终遭遗弃的不幸命运,真切感人。

在魏晋时期,以扇子作为吟咏对象的辞赋作品层出不穷。西晋文人陆机曾经作《羽扇赋》。在赋中,他详细描述了羽扇的雅致之美,使羽扇的地位大大提高。东汉文学家班固作《竹扇赋》,在文中他叙述了竹扇的制作过程、形制、功用,遣词造句通俗易懂。而三国时期的著名诗人曹植,曾经作《九华扇赋》,对皇帝赏赐给他家的一把九华扇大加赞美。

到了诗歌创作繁荣的唐代,引扇子入诗的作品更为丰富。其中有一些诗延续了班婕妤借团扇来抒发宫女哀怨的风格。如杜牧的《秋夕》:"银烛秋光冷画屏,轻罗小扇扑流萤。天阶夜色凉如水,卧看牵牛织女星。"这首诗讲的是:秋天的夜晚,白色的烛光映着冷清的屏风;一个女子手拿绫罗小扇,轻盈地扑打着飞舞的萤火虫。今晚的夜色就如井水般清凉,斜卧在台阶上仰望星空,牵牛星正对着织女星。他借用一把轻罗小扇,将宫中女子孤独寂寞的心情表达了出来。

making process, styles and function. His work was simple and easy to understand. Cao Zhi, a well-known poet in the Three Kingdoms Period once wrote a poem lauding the fan bestowed to him by the emperor.

In the Tang Dynasty when poems began to flourish, there were even more literary works about fans, some of which inherited the style of Ban Jieyu expressing bitterness of palace concubines. An example is Du Mu's poem *Autumn Evening*, which describes a cold autumn evening when a woman looks at Niulang (Altair) and Zhinv

- 《仕女图》吴湖帆(近代)
Portrait of a Lady by Wu Hufan, Modern

中国古代牛郎织女的故事

牛郎织女的故事是一个在中国流传很久的凄美的爱情故事。

传说牛郎从小父母双亡,跟随哥嫂生活。哥嫂对他很不好,整天让他放牛,时间长了他便和老黄牛成为了好朋友。有一天,老黄牛告诉他,天上的织女要和其他仙女一起到凡间来游戏,等她们洗澡的时候你偷偷拿走织女的衣服,那样她就不能回到天上去了。于是牛郎就按照老黄牛说的去做了,结果真的如老黄牛所说,织女就留下来了,并和牛郎结成了夫妻。后来织女为牛郎生下了一儿一女,而老黄牛不久便年老死去了。临死前它告诉牛郎,要留着它的皮,万一遇到紧急的情况就可以拿出来用。

由于织女与牛郎的结合违背了天上的规定,所以王母娘娘知道这件事后,便带领天兵天将来捉拿织女。看到织女就要被王母娘娘捉走,牛郎很是着急,他忽然想到老黄牛临死之前的话,便迅速地找出牛皮,披在身上追上了天。眼看就要追上了,忽然王母娘娘拔下头上的簪子,向银河一划,昔日清浅的银河立刻变得大浪滔

• 清代雕漆牛郎织女纹盒【局部】
画面中牛郎织女隔河相望,一双儿女在牛郎脚下痛哭。
Qing Dynasty Carved Lacquerware Container (partial)
In the painting, Niulang and Zhinv look at each other on each side of the river with tears in their eyes, and their children are crying at the side of Niulang.

天，牛郎再也过不去了。从此，两人只能隔河相望。时间一长，王母娘娘也被他们感动，就准许他们每年七月七日相会一次。相传，每逢七月初七，人间的喜鹊就要飞上天去，在银河搭鹊桥令牛郎织女相会。而古代的女子们就会在这一天仰望天上的牛郎星和织女星，祈祷自己能有一份美满的婚姻。

Ancient Chinese Legend of Niulang and Zhinv

The story of Niulang (the Cowherd) and Zhinv (the Weaving Maid) is a sad and beautiful love story told over thousands of years.

A long time ago, a young cowherd named Niulang lived with his brother and sister-in-law after his parents died. His brother and sister-in-law treated him badly, asking him to herd cows all day and every day. After a while he became a good friend of an old cow. One day, the old cow told him that a weaving maid named Zhinv and six other fairies would come down to earth to play and take bath in the river. If Niulang took away her clothes when she was bathing, Zhinv could no longer return to heaven and had to stay on earth. Niulang did what the old cow told him and eventually married Zhinv, who later gave birth to one son and one daughter. The old cow grew older and older. Before she died, she told Niulang to keep her skin for use in case of emergency.

Because they violated the rule of the heaven, the Goddess of Heaven soon knew about their marriage and came down to earth herself to catch Zhinv. When she was about to be taken away by Goddess of Heaven, Niulang remembered what the old cow told him about the skin. He quickly put on the skin and ran after Zhinv. Before he could catch up with Zhinv, the Goddess of Heaven took out her hairpin and drew a wide, rough river in the sky to separate the couple. They could only watch each other on each side of the river with tears in their eyes. As time went by the Goddess of Heaven was touched by their love. Reluctantly she let them meet once a year on the 7th day of the seventh lunar month. It is said that every year on that day thousands of magpies from the earth flew to the sky to form a bridge on the river so that they could meet on the bridge. Women in ancient times would look at the two stars (Altair representing Niulang and Vega representing Zhinv) praying for a good marriage.

• 牛郎织女鹊桥会
Niulang and Zhinv Meeting at the Magpie Bridge

与杜牧《秋夕》有异曲同工之妙的是宋代词人贺铸写的一首名为《思牛女》的词。在词中他写道："楼角参横，庭心月午。侵阶夜色凉经雨。轻罗小扇扑流萤，微云渡汉思牛女。"这首词可以看作是对杜牧诗的重新演绎，作者也描绘了一幅"轻罗小扇扑流萤"的画面，但是较之《秋夕》，这首词更为通俗易懂。

宋人感情细腻，扇子在他们的笔下更多了一种风情。例如，柳永的《少年游》："世间尤物意中人。轻细好腰身。香帏睡起，发妆酒䣼，红脸杏花春。娇多爱把齐纨扇，和笑掩朱唇。心性温柔，品流闲雅，不称在风尘。"柳永铺垫了一番美人的窈窕身段和动人的妆容，然后说她的娇媚在于用扇子遮住笑颜的样子。绢扇的质地之薄造成了一种半透明的朦胧感觉，所以女子们以这样的扇子来遮面，除尽显羞涩矜持的仪态之外，薄薄的绢扇又使得她们的娇柔羞颜隐隐而露，有"犹抱琵琶半遮面"的风韵和美感。

(Vega) stars while waving a tiny silk fan under a white candle light to pat softly on fireflies. Du Mu fully portrayed a woman's feeling of loneliness with a small fan.

He Zhu, a poet in the Song Dynasty wrote a poem similar to Du Mu's poem *Autumn Evening*. He Zhu's poem *Waving Maid Long for the Cowherd* is pretty much a rewrite of Du Mu's poem in which he described the same scene of "Waving a tiny silk fan under a white candle light to pat softly on fireflies". The only difference was that He Zhu used much simpler words.

Poets of the Song Dynasty were very sensitive about emotions, which added another layer of flavor to fans in their literary works. In his poem *Young Man's Wandering About* he described the slim figure and the lovely look of a beautiful woman and the way she used the fan to cover her smiling face. The thin silk fan leaf produced a translucent effect which women liked to take advantage of in covering their face in the public. The use of silk fan by women in ancient times showed their shy and reserved manner and the charm of their half-hidden beauty as well.

- 《纨扇仕女图》闵贞（清）

  画家着意刻画仕女轻挥纨扇，脉脉含情之态。图中仕女神态娇弱，流露出一种夏日疲困的气息。树干的苍老虬蟠与女子的妩媚身姿，曲线交叉，相映相称，构成新颖别致的格局。

  Painting of Lady with a Silk Fan by Min Zhen, Qing Dynasty (1616-1911)

  The lady in the painting has a fragile body with tenderness in her eyes. She is waving a silk fan lightly showing idleness in a summer day. Her delicate body leaning against an old tree creates a novel and unique image.

除了诗歌之外,中国古典小说之中也常常出现扇子的身影。在古典神话小说《西游记》中,有"孙悟空三调芭蕉扇"的故事。一把普通的芭蕉扇被作者赋予了无穷的能力,它可以熄火、生风,还可以下雨。在历史演义小说《三国演义》中,诸葛亮身披鹤氅,手拿羽扇,坐在四轮车上指挥三军的形象,更是深入人心。在施耐庵的《水浒传》中,"智多星"吴用,手里拿一把"五明扇",显示出其作为军

In addition to poetry, there is often mentioning of fans in the Chinese classical novels. The classic *Journey to the West* tells the story of Monkey King borrowing a palm-leaf fan three times. The fan is described as a magic by the author to put out fire and generate wind and rain. In the classic *Romance of Three Kingdoms*, Zhuge Liang uses his feather fan to command the armies of the three kingdoms on a four-wheel carriage. In the classic *Outlaws of the Marsh*, Wu Yong has a "five wisdom fan" to show his intelligence and stratagems. The

- 《水浒传》中手拿羽扇的吴用
  Outlaws of the Marsh Character Wu Yong Holding a Fan

师的足智多谋。而"浪子"燕青，才貌俱佳，他腰间斜插的一把折扇，更衬托出他的风流倜傥。

在《红楼梦》中，曹雪芹不但描写了折扇、纨扇、芭蕉扇等各式各样的扇子，而且，在他的笔下，扇子已经成为刻画人物、展现人物性格的一种道具。例如，写薛宝钗：有一天，她在滴翠亭看见两

handsome Yan Qing has a folding fan tucked at his waist to demonstrate his elegance and sophistication.

In his novel *Dream of Red Mansions*, Cao Xueqin wrote about a variety of fans such as folding fans, silk fans and palm-leaf fans. Fans were also used as props to portray different characters in his novel. For example, when she saw two butterflies in the garden, Xue Baochai

• 黛玉葬花团扇
Round Fan with Daiyu Flower Funeral Painting

• 《扑蝶图》费以耕（清）
Painting of Catching Butterflies by Fei Yigeng, Qing Dynasty (1616-1911)

只蝴蝶在花间飞舞，不禁童心大发，拿出扇子去扑打蝴蝶。平时的宝钗稳重大方，而扑蝶这一举动，生动地表现了宝钗作为一个女孩天真烂漫的一面。而"晴雯撕扇"的一幕，更是对人物性格最生动的描绘：贾宝玉因心情一直不快，恰巧晴雯帮他换衣时失手把他的扇子跌折。宝玉便训斥了晴雯几句。晴雯的自尊心受到伤害，便还击了一通。宝玉知错，为使晴雯出气，便让晴雯连撕几把扇子来发泄心中的气愤。

此外，以扇子命名的文学作品也很多，其中以清代孔尚任的传奇剧《桃花扇》最为著名。通过明朝末年文人侯方域与秦淮名艳李香君的爱情故事，反映了南明一代兴亡

behaved like a little girl trying to catch them with her fan. Xue was usually a very serious young woman. This moment of playing with butterflies vividly demonstrates the innocent and naive side of her. Another example is the lively description of Qing Wen tearing fans. Qing Wen accidently broke the fan of her master Bao Yu when she was dressing him. Bao Yu was upset and reprimanded Qing Wen, who was so hurt that she fought back. Bao Yu admitted that he was wrong about her and in order to help Qing Wen release her anger he let her tear several of his fans.

There are also literary works named after fans, among which the most famous is the melodrama *Peach Blossom Fan* by Kong Shangren of the Qing Dynasty. The book is about a tragic love story between Hou Fangyu, a scholar and Li Xiangjun, a beauty in the Qinhuai River area in the late Ming Dynasty. A fan is used as a

• 折扇
Folding Fan

的历史。全书以扇子作为线索，把侯方域与李香君的爱情刻画得淋漓尽致。传说在写作该剧时，孔尚任的桌上总放着一把山东特产的缟素扇子，上面画着数朵桃花。每当写到桃花扇时，他都会不由自主地拿起扇子仔细端详一番。

clue throughout the story to illustrate the love between them. It is said that there was always a white silk fan painted with peach blossoms on the desk of the author when he was writing the story. Whenever he wrote the fan he would pick it up and look at it carefully.

● 昆曲《桃花扇》剧照 (图片提供：全景正片)
Still of Kun Opera *Peach Blossom Fan*

《桃花扇》内容简介

　　该剧描写了明末文人侯方域与青楼女子李香君之间曲折的爱情故事。桃花扇在剧中是两人的定情之物。当年落魄的文人侯方域在南京遇到了李香君,两人一见钟情,侯方域题诗扇以赠香君,作为信物。后来由于他人的破坏,侯方域被迫离开南京,李香君也被要求嫁与他人,但她誓死不从,血溅定情诗扇。后来,侯方域的朋友将沾有血迹的扇子点染成一幅桃花,故名桃花扇。

　　该剧将两人的爱情故事放在明代末年动荡的社会背景下,以两人的故事折射出当时社会的现实,具有很强的现实性。

A Brief Summary of Kong Shangren's Melodrama *Peach Blossom Fan*

This is a tortuous love story between Hou Fangyu, a scholar and Li Xiangjun, a courtesan in the late Ming Dynasty. Hou Fanyu fell in love with Li Xiangjun in Nanking when he was still poor and he gave her a fan inscribed with his poem as a token of love between the two. Later Hou was forced to leave Nanking and Li was asked to marry somebody else. Li committed suicide leaving blood drops on the fan, from which Hou's friend painted peach blossoms, hence the name peach blossom fan. The love story taking place during the years of turmoil in the late Ming Dynasty reflects the social reality of that era.

- 文学名著《桃花扇》
  Chinese Classic *Peach Blossom Fan*

> 扇子与戏曲曲艺

> Fans in Chinese Operas and Traditional Art Forms of Quyi

扇子用于戏曲表演，早在宋代的杂剧中就有体现。在戏曲舞台上，扇子成为表现人物身份、彰显人物性格的重要道具。它可以代刀枪，又可以代笔墨。文生可凭借扇子来尽展潇洒，女旦可凭借扇子来

Fans were seen as early as in the Zaju opera of the Song Dynasty (960-1279). Fans became an important stage prop representing swords, knives or pens to demonstrate the character's position and personality. *Sheng* (male roles) use the fan to show their dignified manner; *Dan* (female roles) use the fan to hide their shyness; *Hualian* (painted face roles) use it to add their mightiness; and *Chou* (male clown roles or ugly roles) use it to play

• 宋代杂剧表演中作为道具用的扇子
Zaju Opera Fan Prop of the Song Dynasty (960-1376)

掩遮娇羞，花脸可凭借扇子增添威武，丑角可凭借扇子遍逞滑稽。一把小小的扇子俨然成为戏曲各个行当中的"万能道具"。

funny acts. Fans are an indispensable part of the Chinese opera performances.

京剧中的生、旦、净、末、丑

生，是指戏曲中男性的角色。

旦，是指戏曲中女性的角色。

净，是指脸上画有彩图的花脸角色。"净"是取其反义。

末，是指戏曲中中年男性的角色。他们打头出场，专门为剧情的展开做铺垫。"末"本是末尾的意思，而戏曲中的"末"却是最先上场，这样命名也是取其反义。

丑，是指相貌丑陋、滑稽可笑的人物。他们最明显的标志是在鼻子处画有一大块白。

• 老旦 文丑
Laodan (Elderly Female Role) and Wenchou (Civilian Comic Role)

• 老生 花旦
Laosheng (Elderly Male Role) and Huadan (Young Female Role)

Sheng, *Dan*, *Jing*, *Mo* and *Chou* Roles in Peking Operas

Sheng refers to male roles in the opera.

Dan refers to female roles in the opera.

Jing refers to painted face male roles. Jing means "clean" in Chinese. The Jing role means the opposite of cleanness.

Mo refers to middle-aged male roles. They usually come out first to prepare for the start of the drama. Mo means the end in Chinese. But in a Chinese opera, a Mo role always comes out first. So the name of the role also means the opposite of Mo.

Chou roles are ugly and comical. Their most standout feature is a small patch of white chalk around the nose.

戏曲舞台上经常使用的有折扇、团扇、羽扇、芭蕉扇、竹扇、掌扇、鹅毛扇。不同形式的扇子，配予不同身份、不同性格的角色使用。一般帝王、皇后出场，是用龙凤掌扇代替銮驾。小姐、丫鬟用团

Fans frequently used in the Chinese operas include folding fans, round fans, feather fans, palm-leaf fans, bamboo fans, ceremonial palm fans and goose feather fans. Different types of fans represent roles of different social status and different personalities. When kings or queens come out on the stage, ceremonial palm fans painted with dragons or phoenixes are used to function as the imperial carriage; misses and their maids use round fans; servants and bearers use palm leaf fans; and court advisors always hold feather fans. The most

- 扇子在戏曲中的应用
  The Usage of Fan in Chinese Operas

● 扇子生（图片提供：全景正片）
Fan Sheng

扇；差役、轿夫用蒲扇；谋士、军师则持羽扇。在众多的扇子当中尤以折扇的使用最广泛，生旦净末丑各个行当都能用到。

在京剧之中还有一个行当称为"扇子生"。"扇子生"分为两类。一类是扮相知书达理、文质彬彬的儒雅书生，一扇在手，风度翩翩。还有一类是方巾丑，头上戴着方巾，身穿褶子衣，手里摇着扇子，也是文人扮相，但略带一些迂腐气，给人一种滑稽的感觉。

戏曲中的扇子功是体现演员基本功的重要形式，被列为戏曲表演的基本功之一。扇子功的基本动作有挥、转、托、夹、合、遮、扑、

commonly used are folding fans, which are appropriate for any role (*Sheng*, *Dan*, *Jin*, *Mo* and *Chou*) in the Chinese operas.

There are two types of *"Shanzisheng"* roles(male roles carrying fan) in Peking opera. One has an appearance of a gentle, knowledgeable scholar holding a stylish fan. The other wears a square scarf on the head and a creasy shirt, also holding a fan, but giving an impression of a bookish, comic character.

The fan performance is one of the basic trainings in the Chinese operas. How a performer uses a fan demonstrates how well he or she is trained. The techniques include waving, turning, holding, clipping, closing, covering, fluttering, shaking and throwing of a fan.

抖、抛等。通过这些基本动作，配合演员的身段，能衍化出各种舞姿，耍出各种花式，形成各种用扇程式，用以表现人物的情绪，刻画人物的性格。《贵妃醉酒》中，京剧表演艺术大师梅兰芳借助一柄折叠扇，把杨贵妃的婀娜醉态表演得出神入化。在《失空斩》中，诸葛亮就通过扇子的摇、顿、颤、抖，表现出自己面对司马懿兵临空城下的内心紧张，以及对马谡不听嘱咐致使街亭失守的愤怒和遗憾。

Together with the actor's posture, these techniques can produce great varieties of dance movements and fanning patterns to best illustrate emotions and individualities of different opera characters. In the Peking Opera *The Drunken Beauty*, the grand master of Peking Opera Mei Lanfang gave a superb performance of mellow drunkenness of Palace Concubine Yang with a help of a folding fan. In the Peking Opera series *Lost, Empty, Behead*, the key character Zhuge Liang shows his nervousness in implementing his scheme of an empty city in face of enemy and his anger towards his general Ma Su, who lost Jieting by using different fan performances of waving, stomping, shaking and shivering.

- 京剧《贵妃醉酒》
  Peking Opera *The Drunken Beauty*

京剧《贵妃醉酒》《失空斩》简介

京剧《贵妃醉酒》讲的是唐玄宗与他的贵妃杨玉怀之间的故事。有一次，唐玄宗答应与杨玉环一同饮酒赏花，但是当天唐玄宗却没有赴约。于是杨玉环很生气，便独自饮酒排遣忧愁。不一会儿她便喝醉了，京剧《贵妃醉酒》重点表现的就是她喝醉之后独自赏春的心态。

此剧是京剧大师梅兰芳的代表作品，他通过外形动作的变化来表现人物从内心苦闷、强自作态到不能自制、沉醉失态的心理变化过程，细腻生动，令人叫绝。

京剧《失空斩》是一组传统京剧曲目《失街亭》《空城计》《斩马谡》的合称。因为三出戏在内容上相互衔接，所以被简称为《失空斩》。

该剧讲述的是三国时期诸葛亮率军北伐的故事。当时蜀国与魏国交战，魏军攻打蜀国的咽喉要地街亭，将军马谡请求前去防守。临行前诸葛亮再三叮嘱他一定要慎重，但是由于马谡的疏忽，最后还是失守街亭。于是魏军乘胜直取西城，由于之前西城官兵都已经调遣在外，诸葛亮只好使用空城计，将城门大开，独坐城楼，故作镇定。魏军将领因怀疑其城内有重兵埋伏而撤兵，西城最终得以保住。而马谡由于犯了重大的过失罪而被斩首。

● 杨柳青年画《杨妃醉酒》
The Drunken Beauty a Woodblock Painting of Yangliuqing, Tianjin

Brief Summaries of *The Drunken Beauty* and *the Series Lost, Empty, Behead*

The Drunken Beauty tells the story between the Tang Emperor Xuanzong and his favorite palace concubine Yang Yuhuan. Once he promised Yang to drink wine in a flower garden, but he never showed up. Yang was so upset that she started to drink alone to drive away her sadness. The opera shows her state of mind after she was drunk.

This opera is a representation of Peking Opera master Mei Lanfang's repertoire. His portrayal of the changing gestures and attitudes from bitterness to uncontrollable drunkenness of the concubine was superbly convincing and widely acclaimed.

Lost, Empty, Behead is an abbreviation of three consecutive Peking Operas *Lost Jieting, Scheme of Empty City* and *Behead Ma Su*.

This opera series tells the story of the northern expedition led by Zhuge Liang during the Three Kingdoms Period. In the battle between State Shu and State Wei, Shu general Ma Su was asked to defend the key stronghold Jieting against the Wei army. Before he left for Jieting, Zhuge Liang kept telling him to be very careful. But he eventually lost Jieting to Wei due to his negligence. As a result, the Wei army was marching towards Xicheng (West City) of Shu when most of Shu armies had been sent away. Zhuge Liang had to use a scheme by opening the city gate and sitting at the top of the gate pretending to be very calm to fool the Wei army. The Wei generals mistakenly thought that there was massive ambush inside the city and decided to withdraw. Zhuge Liang successfully protected the city alone and the Shu general Ma Su was beheaded for his gross negligence.

梅兰芳与扇子

据说京剧大师梅兰芳在表演《晴雯撕扇》时，一定会在上台之前，先亲笔精心画一张扇面，装上扇骨，带到台上去表演，然后当场撕掉。演一次、画一次、撕一次，这已经成了规律。

梅兰芳热衷收藏书画扇，其中大多是竹扇，唯有一把是圆形的绢面纳扇。这把扇子是1924年5月，印度诗人泰戈尔在看了梅兰芳演出的《洛神》后亲手所赠。扇面上有泰戈尔用毛笔书写的孟加拉文和英文的即兴题诗。

Mei Langfang and Fans

It is said that before he performed *Qing Wen Tearing the Fan*, the Peking Opera master Mei Lanfang would personally paint the fan leaf and install the fan stick. He would tear the fan during his performance. It became his practice to paint and tear the fan in each of his performances of that opera.

Mei Langfang liked to collect fans with paintings and calligraphies. Most of the fans in his collection are bamboo fans, except one round white silk fan, which was given to him as a gift by Indian poet Rabindranath Tagore after Tagore saw Mei's performance in *Nymph of River Lo*. The fan has Tagore's spontaneous poem inscribed in both English and Bengali.

京剧大师梅兰芳
Peking Opera Master Mei Lanfang

除了戏曲之外，其他曲艺表演中也经常使用扇子。例如，在相声表演的舞台上，扇子是必备的道具之一，相声表演中有"打哏"这一术语，即在表演中，一个人要不时地用扇子来打另一个人，以此来逗人发笑。

传统的相声表演是由捧哏演员与逗哏演员两个人共同完成的。逗哏演员是叙述故事的主要演员，他要不断说出笑料以使得观众发笑。而捧哏演员要对逗哏演员所说的话

In addition to being used in opera, fans are also frequently used in Quyi. For example, fans are necessary stage props in Chinese crosstalk (*Xiangsheng*). There is a specific technical term in the Chinese crosstalk called *Dagen*, in which one comedian hits the other comedian with a fan to amuse the audience.

Traditional Chinese crosstalk usually involves two performers. One is the comic who delivers the lines that make the audience laugh while the other plays a supporting role to respond to the main

相声演员手中的扇子
Fans Used by Chinese Crosstalk Performers

清代评书演员柳敬亭画像
Portrait of Liu Jingting, a Chinese Storyteller in the Qing Dynasty (1616-1911)

表示一定的态度，是对逗哏演员所说内容的一种补充和铺垫，一般捧哏演员的话语比较简短。在以"打哏"为主的相声中，逗哏演员就会找出各种理由来用扇子去打捧哏演员，而观众看到捧哏演员有苦说不出的尴尬局面，便会忍不住捧腹大笑。

扇子也是评书演员必备的道具。评书也是曲艺的一种形式，就是由一个人口述故事。评书演员在叙事过程中，要不断模拟场景，变

comic to carry on the dialogue. Usually the words from the supporting comic are short and simple. In the cross talk with *Dagen* as the main style, the main comic would find all kinds of excuses to hit the supporting comic with a fan to make the audience laugh at the awkwardness of the supporting comic.

Fans are also a necessary stage prop in Chinese storytelling, which is basically a monologue. The story-teller uses the fan to simulate different scenes and to change from one character to another. Therefore,

换角色，这时扇子就会随着叙事内容的变化而被赋予不同的性能。例如，在讲到打斗场景时，演员就要将扇子作为兵器，模拟出战斗的情景；讲到书写的情景时，扇子就要变成一杆笔，刷刷点点，表现写出了锦绣文章。正所谓"醒木一敲风雷动，折扇轻摇论古今"，一把折扇，使评书演员的表演变得栩栩如生。

a fan can play different roles based on the changes in the story. For example, when the story is about fighting, the storyteller would use the fan as a weapon to simulate a fighting scene. When the story is about writing, the fan would become a pen that the story character uses to write an article. A folding fan can make the performance of a storyteller true to life.

• 龙凤折扇
Folding Fan with Dragon and Phoenix Paintings

说书人所用扇子的来历

评书演员在表演时,总是放一把扇子在桌面上,传说这一习俗与清朝的乾隆皇帝有关。

乾隆下江南微服私访。一日他来到一座桥上,忽然诗性大发,随口吟出一首诗:"朕在桥上观四方,四方,四方,四四方。""我在桥下呼万岁,万岁,万岁,万万岁。"桥下有人答道。乾隆一下愣住了:桥下何人能把我的诗对答如流?他往下一看,原来是一位老叟光着脚丫站在桥下钓鱼。乾隆忙叫人把桥下这位老叟请上来。

原来老叟是一位说书人,于是乾隆和这位老叟交了朋友,想让他做官并送给他金子,但都被老叟谢绝了。于是乾隆临走时送给老叟一把扇子,提笔在扇子上写到:"朕于江南走,桥下遇老叟。原是说书人,与我交朋友。赏官他不做,赠金也不收。持把风凉扇,便于天下游。逢县县官接,逢州州官留。哪个敢不从,定斩颈上头。"老叟接过扇子谢过皇帝,继续说他的书去了。

这件事传开后,所有的说书人都效仿老叟也拿着一把扇子。

- 启功《万松图》泥金折扇

Gilded Folding Fan with *Painting Pine Trees* by Qi Gong (1912-2005)

Origin of the Storyteller's Fan

A Chinese storyteller always places a fan on the table when he performs. It is said that this tradition is related to Emperor Qianlong of the Qing Dynasty.

During his unofficial visit to the south of the Yangtze River, one day Emperor Qianlong suddenly had an urge to chant a poem spontaneously on a bridge. When he said, "I am looking at the expansive view of my country on the bridge", a person under the bridge responded immediately, "I am chanting for the long life of your Majesty under the bridge." Emperor was surprised that some guy could finish his couplet so well. He saw a bare-foot old man fishing under the bridge and asked him to come up on the bridge.

It turned out that he was a storyteller, who came to fish during his break. The emperor and the old man became friends. The emperor wanted the old man to become his court official and give him some gold, but his offers were refused by the old man. Before leaving, the emperor gave him a fan and wrote a poem for him, which said, "I met an old man while visiting south of Yantze River; he is a storyteller and we become friends; he doesn't want to be a court official and he doesn't accept my gold; he wants to travel around the earth with a fan in hand; he should be welcomed by the county and state court officials; if he is not well-treated, I'll behead the officials." The old man thanked the emperor for the fan and continued with his story telling tours.

The story had then been widely circulated, and all storytellers followed the old man and carried a fan with them.

• 折扇
Folding Fan

> 扇子与舞蹈

历史上有先民"操牛尾,歌八阕"的记载。自扇子问世之后,舞者便将扇子编入舞蹈动作当中,于是"扇舞"应时而生,扇子便也成为中国传统舞蹈中最富有表现性和情感特质的道具之一。

将扇子纳入舞蹈当中,大大增加了舞姿的优美性,舞者或者以

> Fans in Dances

The Chinese are good at singing and dancing. When fans came into being, Chinese dancers choreographed them into dance movements and fans became props in the Chinese traditional dances.

Fans in dances add artistry and elegance. The dancer can use the fan to cover her face or dance with the fan. Each dance movement with the fan

• 舞蹈用扇
A Dance Fan

● 持扇跳舞的女子（图片提供：FOTOE）
Dancers with Fans

扇掩面，或者持扇起舞，举手投足之间，一种含蓄蕴藉之美展露无遗。传说魏晋南北朝时期，有一个名叫绿珠的女子，精通音律，尤其善于持扇跳舞，以至于当时人们都称她所持的扇子为"歌扇"。歌者手拿一柄扇子，边唱边跳，轻薄的舞衣借助扇子的灵巧，能够塑造出更美的舞姿。北朝诗人庾信就曾作诗云："绿珠歌扇薄，飞燕舞袖长。"将绿珠与西汉时期的赵飞燕相提并论，可见，绿珠持扇舞蹈的

shows an implicit beauty. It is said that during the Wei, Jin and Southern and Northern dyhasties, a woman named Lv Zhu was very good at music and dancing, especially fan dancing. People called her fan "singing fan". She always sang and danced with a fan in her hand. Her light dancing costume with an exquisite fan made her movement even more attractive. Yu Xin, a poet of the Northern dynasties compared Lv Zhu's singing fan dances to another well-known dancer Zhao Feiyan in the Western Han Dynasty in his poem

赵飞燕人物介绍

赵飞燕是西汉时期汉成帝的皇后，因为她舞姿轻盈，如同燕子飞舞，故此被称为"飞燕"。传说她能在盘子上跳舞，可见其体态之轻盈。有一次汉成帝命人手托水晶盘，让赵飞燕在盘中跳舞，只见晶莹的盘上，一个灵动的身躯翩翩起舞，汉成帝很是欢喜。后来，人们将这件事夸大，变成了她能在掌心中跳舞。

Introduction of Zhao Feiyan

Zhao Feiyan (meaning flying swallow) was the Empress of Emperor Cheng of the Western Han Dynasty. She danced so well just like a flying swallow and people called her Feiyan. It is said that she was so light that she could dance on a plate. According to a legend, Emperor Cheng asked a court maid to place a crystal plate on her hand and let Zhao dance on it. Zhao did beautifully and the emperor liked it very much. Later the story was so exaggerated that it turned into her dancing on a hand palm.

- 清人所绘赵飞燕图

Painting of Zhao Feiyan by an Artist in the Qing Dynasty (1616-1911)

姿态是多么优美。

在唐代大型宫廷舞蹈《霓裳羽衣舞》中，扇子的巧妙运用，则生动地表现了缥缈的仙境。该舞蹈以杨贵妃的领舞和嫔妃们的表演而著名。在舞蹈的开端，一群身着洁白

- 《瑶池霓裳图》任薰（清）
Painting of Fairy Gatherings at Yaochi, Residence of Goddess Mother by Ren Xun, Qing Dynasty (1616-1911)

describing the lightness of her singing fan dances as beautiful as the flying dancing sleeves of Zhao.

In the large court dance *Colorful Feather Costume Dance* of the Tang Dynasty (618-907), fans were used cleverly to present an ethereal wonderland. The dance became famous when it was led by Palace Concubine Yang with participations of other court ladies. In the beginning of the dance, Yang was hidden in the center by a group of dancers dressed in white costumes with peacock feather fans. Then fans gradually receded and Yang appeared dancing in a long chiffon dress. Her dance movements became faster and faster spinning and leaping like a blooming white lotus. When he saw *the Colorful Feather Costume Dance* performance, Bai Juyi, the famous poet of the Tang Dynasty said in his poem, "Of countless songs and dances I love the colorful feather costume dance the best."

The classical solo dance *Spring Moonlight over Blossoms by the River* produced in 1950s is as unique as the *Colorful Feather Costume Dance*. This dance shows a young woman seeing spring blossoms along the river under the moonlight that makes her yearn for a

《霓裳羽衣曲》的由来

　　《霓裳羽衣舞》是根据《霓裳羽衣曲》的曲调来表演的。《霓裳羽衣曲》传说是由唐玄宗从月宫中听来的。中秋月圆的时候，一个叫罗公远的道士引领着唐玄宗来到了月宫。在月宫中，唐玄宗见到很多仙女在乐曲声中翩翩起舞，便询问仙女们演奏的曲子是什么。一个仙女回答说是"霓裳羽衣"。通晓音乐的唐玄宗于是默默地记住了这个曲子的曲调。等返回皇宫之后，他便立刻将在月宫中听到的曲子写了下来。但是他仅仅能回忆起此曲的一半曲调。正好当时有人进献了一首《婆罗门曲》，其曲调与唐玄宗在月宫中所听到的很相似。于是唐玄宗便以在月宫中听到的曲调为"散序"，以进献来的《婆罗门曲》为"散序"之后的乐章，并定名为《霓裳羽衣曲》。

The Origin of *Colorful Feather Costume Melody*

Colorful Feather Costume Dance came from *Colorful Feather Costume Melody*, which is said to be music Emperor Xuanzong of the Tang Dynasty heard in the moon palace. During the Moon Festival, a Taoist priest named Luo Gongyuan led the emperor to the moon palace where he saw fairies dancing to this melody. So he asked them what it was and they told him that it was the *Colorful Feather Costume Melody*. Emperor Xuanzong was very good at music, so he remembered the tune. After he was back to his palace, he wrote down the tune immediately. But he only remembered half of it. Accidentally, someone just presented him a *Brahman* Sangeet, which sounded very similar to what he heard in the moon palace. So Emperor Xuanzong used the tune he heard from the moon palace as the prelude and the *Brahman* Sangeet for the rest of the music movements. He then officially named the melody *Colorful Feather Costume Melody*.

▶ 吹笛子的唐玄宗
Emperor Xuanzong of the Tang Dynasty Playing a Chinese Flute

舞裙，手持孔雀扇的舞女用扇子将中间的杨贵妃隐藏起来。随着乐曲的展开，扇子渐渐退去，只见杨贵妃身着薄纱长裙，翩翩起舞。随着乐曲的节奏由慢逐渐变快，杨贵妃的动作也逐渐变快，旋转着，跳跃着，犹如一朵绽放的白莲花。后来

bright future. The dancer in a blue chiffon dress has a white feather fan in each hand. She dances like a flying butterfly around flowers expressing her longings for love and a better life. In the end, she turns away and disappears in a misty fog adding a feeling of mystery to the dance.

Chinese folk dances also use fans

• 手拿羽扇跳舞的女子
Dancing Woman with Feather Fans

著名诗人白居易在观赏过《霓裳羽衣舞》后，赞叹道："千歌万舞不可数，就中最爱霓裳舞。"

创作于20世纪50年代的古典独舞《春江花月夜》与《霓裳羽衣舞》有异曲同工之妙。舞蹈表现的是在一个春天的夜晚，一位少女漫步在江边，面对着满眼的春色，不由得生发出对未来美好的憧憬。舞蹈开场，舞者身着一袭蓝色的纱裙，手中持一对洁白的羽扇走上舞台。她犹如一只翩翩起舞的蝴蝶，伴着悠扬的旋律，时而萦绕于花丛中，时而停留在枝头上。她眼波流转，脉脉含情，将一个少女对爱情和美好生活的向往表现得淋漓尽致。舞蹈最后，舞者在一个旋转坐地之后，消失在一片雾霭之中，为舞蹈平添了一份神秘与缥缈的美感。

除了古典舞蹈外，在中国的民间舞蹈中也经常可以看到扇子的身影。例如，秧歌，原本是农民在插秧时的一种歌咏活动，后来发展成为乐舞结合的表演形式，并流行于全国各地。著名的东北大秧歌，表演者手持扇子、手帕、彩绸等道具，身体随着锣鼓点儿不断地颤、摇、转、拧、仰、俯、屈、伸。一把红

such as in the Yangge dance, which was originally a singing activity among peasants during the crop planting season. Later it evolved into a musical form with both dancing and singing and became very popular all over China. In the famous Yangge in Northeast of China, dancers use fans, handkerchiefs and colorful silk ribbons. They shake, swing, and turn the fans moving their bodies to the drum beat to express their happiness.

Fans are also an important prop in the tea picking folk dance in the south of the Yangtze River. In the performance,

● 秧歌闹元宵 (图片提供：FOTOE)
Yangge Performance during the Lantern Festival

火的绸扇不断翻转，营造出一种欢快、热烈的氛围。

在广泛流行于江南地区的采茶舞中，扇子也是最重要的道具。表演过程中，舞者一手提竹篮，一手持彩扇。为了能表现出欢快的气氛，表演者要挥动扇子，不断舞出美妙的扇花。

在少数民族的舞蹈中，也常常使用扇子。朝鲜族的"扇子舞"是具有鲜明朝鲜族特色的舞蹈。表演中，舞者身穿白衣，手持羽扇，

the dancers have a bamboo basket in one hand and a colorful fan in the other. They use the fan to create different movements demonstrating a cheerful and happy atmosphere.

Fans are frequently used in dances of Chinese ethnic groups as well. The fan dance of China's Korean ethnic group has its distinctive characteristics. The dancer in white clothes imitates a flying silver pheasant using a feather fan to demonstrate a peaceful life in the countryside. The Hani ethnic group in

● 朝鲜扇子舞 (图片提供：全景正片)
Fan Dancing of China's Korean Ethnic Group

- 檀香扇
Sandalwood Fan

模仿白鹇飞翔的姿态，韵律优美、柔和，表现出一派宁静、自由的农林生活。云南的哈尼族有"棕扇舞"，舞蹈者手拿着棕榈叶，在优美舒缓的乐曲的伴奏下翩翩起舞。

扇子在舞者手中被赋予了新的生机与活力，舞蹈由于扇子的辉映变得更加多姿，两者相辅相成，各显其美。

Yunnan province dances with a brown palm-leaf fan.

Fans in the hands of dancers become livelier and dances with the use of fans become more colorful. Each has its own beauty and one is complementary to the other.

中国古典名曲《春江花月夜》简介

《春江花月夜》是一首琵琶独奏曲,至今已有一千多年的历史。它的原名为《夕阳箫鼓》,后来人们根据唐代诗人白居易《琵琶行》中"浔阳江头夜送客"的诗句,将其更名为《浔阳曲》《浔阳夜月》,1930年正式定名为《春江花月夜》。

乐曲描写的是春天静谧的夜晚,月亮在东山升起,花影在岸堤摇曳,一叶扁舟在江面荡漾,而远处隐隐传来箫鼓之声,使人沉湎于这诗情画意之中……

全曲共分为十个小的段落,每一段都有不同的标题:《江楼钟鼓》《月上东山》《风回水转》《花影层台》《水深云际》《渔歌唱晚》《回澜拍岸》、《桡鸣远濑》《欸乃归舟》《尾声》。

Brief Introduction of Chinese Traditional Music
Spring Moonlight over Blossoms by the River

Spring Moonlight over Blossoms by the River is a Pipa (Chinese lute) solo piece with over a thousand years of history. The original name was *Music at the Sunset*. Later the name was changed to *Xunyang Melody* or *Moonlight in Xunyang* based on a verse ("Seeing off a guest at night by the Xunyang River") in the poem *Ode of Pipa* by the poet Bai Juyi of the Tang Dynasty. In 1930, the name was set as *Spring Moonlight over Blossoms by the River*.

The music describes tranquility of a spring night when the moon rises from the mountain in the east casting shadows of flowers along the river with a small boat floating on ripples of water and music faintly heard from afar. The music engages people in a romantic mood.

There are ten short movements in the music each having a different poetic title:
Bells and Drums on the River Tower
Moon Rises in East Mountain
Wind Returns the Backwater
Shadows of Flowers on Terrace
Deep Water and Distant Clouds
Fishermen Singing at Dusk
Waves Splash the Shorelines
Sound of Paddles against Rushing Water
Boats Return to Shore
Coda

> 扇子与园林建筑

中国古代园林建筑蕴含着深厚的中国文化底蕴，建筑者把对美的理解运用到建筑物之上。而中国古代的折扇由于在形制结构上精美雅致，加上历代文人对它所赋予的文化内涵，自然被建筑设计者所关注。无

> Fans in Landscape Architecture

The Chinese classical landscape architecture involves the profound influence of Chinese culture. The Chinese craftsmen apply their understanding of aesthetics to landscape structures. The ancient folding fans have a beautiful and elegant shape and structure, and great literary implications thanks to scholars and poets in different dynasties. Therefore architects tend to have a strong interest in them. Fan-shaped structures can be found in imperial gardens as well

• 山西王家大院墙上的扇洞
Fan-Shaped Window on the Wall of Wang's Grand Courtyard, Shanxi Province

• 扇形木雕
Fan-shaped Carved Wood Decoration

论是皇家园林，还是普通民居，折扇造型的建筑随处可见。

在著名的苏州园林里，矗立着一座折扇形的凉亭。它位于拙政园东南角，东南朝向，后是小山，前临清泉，环境幽静。凉亭的屋面、轩门、窗洞、石桌、石凳及轩顶、灯罩、墙上匾额、鹅颈椅、半栏都呈扇面状，于是当地人都亲切地称呼它为"扇亭"。其实这座亭子有一个雅致的名字——"与谁同坐轩"，取自宋代著

as gardens of private residencies.

A fan-shaped pavilion is situated in the southeastern corner of the Humble Administrator's Garden, one of the renowned Suzhou Gardens. With a small hill behind and a pond in the front, the pavilion sits in a peaceful environment. Its roof, door, window lattices, stone tables, stone stools, corridor ceilings, lampshades, the inscribed board on the wall, gooseneck chairs and handrails were all built in the fan-leaf shape. The

● 苏州园林中的扇亭
Fan-Shaped Pavilion in a Suzhou Garden

● 苏州园林扇亭内景
The Interior of the Fan-shaped Pavilion in a Suzhou Garden

名词人苏东坡的词句"与谁同坐，明月清风我"。

亭子的主人是清代人张履谦。他是一个富裕的商人，中年时定居苏州，并建造了这座亭子。因为他的祖上是靠卖扇子起家的，所以在建造亭子的时候，为了铭记祖上创业的艰辛，就将亭子的形状建造成了折扇的样子。

"与谁同坐轩"体现的是主人高雅的品性，而皇家园林中的扇形建筑更多体现的是儒家的仁义精神。

坐落在北京颐和园西面的扇面殿——"扬仁风"，就是将儒家仁义

locals call it "Fan Pavilion". Its official name is the "With Whom Shall I Sit" Pavilion based on the verses (With whom can I sit? The bright moon, a light breeze and myself.) from the famous poet Su Dongpo of the Song Dynasty.

The owner of this pavilion was Zhang Lvqian, a wealthy businessman in the Qing Dynasty. He settled down in Suzhou during his middle-age years and built this pavilion. His ancestors made a living on selling fans. So he built this fan-shaped pavilion in memory of the hard work of his family's previous generations.

The "With Whom Shall I Sit" Pavilion shows the elegant character of its owner. In the imperial gardens, fan-shaped structures on the other hand demonstrate the spirit of benevolence of Confucianism.

A typical example is the fan-shaped hall called "Wind of Virtue" in the west side of the Summer Palace in Beijing. The name itself shows how Confucianism was

• 北京颐和园中的扇面殿——扬仁风
Hall of Wind of Virtue in Fan Shape in the Summer Palace, Beijing

• 北京天坛公园扇面亭
Fan-Shaped Pavilion in the Temple of Heaven, Beijing

精神运用到建筑上的一个典型例子。这一点单从它的名字"扬仁风"上就能够体现出来。当年东晋宰相谢安在送好友袁宏远行时,将一把扇子作为礼物送给他,希望他能够弘扬仁义之风,而清朝统治者正是借用了这一典故来为扇面殿命名,以此来表现他们的仁爱之心。

此殿始建于清代乾隆年间,地面呈扇面形,殿前地面的石条成扇骨形,有汉白玉雕成的扇轴,整个殿的平面就像一把展开的折扇。此

applied to the concept of the structure. In the East Jin Dynasty (317-420), the prime minister Xie An gave his friend Yuan Hong a fan as a farewell gift hoping that he would continue to promote Confucius virtues. The ruling class of the Qing Dynasty named it "Wind of Virtue" based on this reference to demonstrate their benevolence.

This hall was built in the Emperor Qianlong's reign of the Qing Dynasty. The floor in the hall was built in the shape of a fan leaf paved with stone bars in the shape of fan sticks and a white

外，殿内的宝座、香几、宫灯均呈扇面形。由于在一座建筑之中有着这么多扇形的结构，人们因之称它为"扇面殿"。

北京北海公园中的"延南薰"也是一个扇形结构的亭子。它位于北海琼华岛塔山的北面，亭子不大，一共三间。亭子前边有一个月台，月台像扇子逐渐缩窄，呈三角形，形成了一个扇子的骨架。而三角形上的扇骨是用石头镶嵌出来的，在扇骨交叉的地方，有一个圆形的浮雕就是扇轴。亭子取名为"延南薰"，是根据古代传说中舜帝发明五弦琴，并谱写了"延南薰曲"而来的。这座亭子也建于清代乾隆年间，传说当年乾隆皇帝经常来这里练习武术。因为他身上经常佩带一把折扇，建筑工匠就据此修建了这座凉亭。

carved marble shaft. The entire layout of the hall resembles an open folding fan. In addition, the throne, incent burners and palace lanterns are all in the shape of a fan leaf. People call it "Fan-Shaped Hall" because of so many fan-shaped objects in one architecture.

There is another fan-shaped pavilion called *Yannanxun* situated north of Qionghua Islet in Beihai Park in Beijing. It is a small pavilion with three structures. In the front of the pavilion is a veranda built in a triangle fan shape. The fan sticks are stone mosaic with a round relief as the fan shaft. The pavilion's name came from an ancient legend about a five-string Chinese banjo invented by Emperor Shun and the music composed by him. This pavilion was also built in Emperor Qianlong's reign. It is said that he often came here to practice martial arts and he always carried a folding fan with him. The craftsmen build it based on this habit of Emperor Qianlong.

> 扇子与民俗礼仪

在中国悠久的历史中，使用扇子的过程中形成了许多有趣的风俗。

在中国古代有端午节送扇子的习俗。古人认为端午节送扇子可以

• 清代双仕女年画
New Year Painting of Two Ladies, Qing Dynasty (1616-1911)

> Fans in Folk Customs and Etiquettes

In the long history of China, the use of fans has helped to form many interesting customs.

In ancient China people had a tradition of giving fans as gifts in the Dragon Boat Festival to repel evils. Because Dragon Boat Festival took place between late spring and early summer, mosquitoes and insects started to come out. Calamus and mugwort were used as disinfection herbs and help to ward off these insects. Therefore people gave a fan as a gift together with calamus and mugwort. Fans were known as the "disease repellent fans" in those days. As early as in the Tang Dynasty, Emperor

辟邪。端午节有饮雄黄酒，插艾蒿的风俗。因为端午正值春夏之交，容易滋生各种蚊虫，此时用艾草、菖蒲来消毒，能起到很好的防虫防蝇的作用。将扇子与其他辟邪的物品一起送的目的也是为了避瘟疫，故此扇子也有"避瘟扇"之称。早在唐代，唐太宗就曾在端午节送扇子给大臣。时至今日，在浙江杭州萧山地区，端午节仍旧有这样一个习俗：姑娘出嫁的第一年，娘家人要带着编好的麦草扇去看望新出嫁的姑娘，而姑娘则要把扇子分赠给婆家的亲戚。在盛产羽扇的湖州农

Taizong bestowed fans on his ministers in the Dragon Boat Festival. Even at the present day in Xiaoshan District, Hangzhou in Zhejiang province, a young woman should distribute fans to the relatives of her husband's family during the Dragon Boat Festival in her first year of marriage. In the rural areas of Huzhou where feather fans are made, there is a similar tradition today where the bride has to bring a feather fan with other gifts to her mother-in-law's family in her first visit in Dragon Boart Festival.

In ancient China traditional wedding ceremonies had a custom of "taking the fan off". Before the start of the custom

• 《意在笔先》吴嘉猷（清）
Painting of Thinking before Painting by Wu Jiayou, Qing Dynasty (1616-1911)

• 执扇的新娘
Bride Holding a Fan

村地区，也有一个类似的风俗，即新娘在端午节第一次去婆家，所带的礼物中一定要有一把羽毛扇。

在中国古代传统的婚嫁习俗中，还有"却扇"这一风俗。在蒙在新娘头上的盖头出现以前，女子出嫁时要用扇子遮住脸，一直要等到进入洞房后才能由新郎将扇子移去。这种风俗在南北朝时已经形成。南朝刘义庆的《世说新语》有记载：晋人温峤的姑母让温峤为她的女儿挑选丈夫。后来温峤替姑母选好了女婿。等到婚礼进行时，由于新娘急于想知道新郎是谁，就自己用手拨开扇子，结果受到了当时人们的嘲笑。到了唐代，不仅有新娘用扇"掩面"，新郎还有"却

of wearing a veil, the bride had to cover her face with a fan in the wedding, which could only be removed by her husband. This already became a custom in the Southern and Northern dynasties (420-589). In a note by Liu Yiqing of the Southern dynasties, Wen Qiao in the Jin Dynasty selected the husband for his cousin at his aunt's request. During the wedding, the bride was so eager to see who the groom was that she took off the fan herself. As a result people laughed at her. In the Tang Dynasty, there were customs for the bride to cover her face with a fan and for the groom to remove the fan. The groom had to write a poem about removing the fan before he actually did it. In the historical records, Emperor Zhongzong of the Tang Dynasty asked

● 婚礼坐帐
Wedding Night

扇"（即除去扇子的意思）的习俗。而且新郎在拿开新娘面前的扇子之前，要作"却扇诗"。据史料记载：唐中宗的妹妹出嫁时，他就曾经令大臣作却扇诗。唐代著名的诗人李商隐还曾经作为伴郎，替新郎作过却扇诗。由此可见这一习俗在当时的流行程度。

有些地方的婚俗中，新郎手中也拿着一把扇子，不过这把扇子的用场却和新娘的大不相同。新娘用扇子来遮羞，而新郎主要是用扇子

his minister to write a removing fan poem at his sister's wedding. Li Shangyin, a well-known poet in the Tang Dynasty, wrote a fan poem for the groom when he was the best man. It is evident that it was a very popular custom in ancient China.

In some areas, the groom also carried a fan in the wedding. Unlike the bride's fan, the groom first used it to knock lightly at the door of the sedan chair for three times before the door was opened and the bride stepped down. Secondly as soon as the bride was out, the groom

作为敲轿门、挑盖头的工具。在新娘下轿前,新郎先用扇子在轿门上轻敲三下,然后由娶亲的人启开轿门。新娘下轿后,新郎马上由伴郎扶着登高,并用合着的扇子在新娘头顶上轻打三下,及至拜过天地后,再用扇子挑去新娘蒙头盖面的"盖头",到此,婚礼才算完成。

would go to a higher place with the help of his best man using a closed folding fan to lightly pat on the bride's head. After they paid respects to their parents and deities, the groom would use the fan to raise the veil the bride wore over her head to complete the wedding ceremony.

- 刺绣作品——喜上眉梢
  Embroidery: Magpies on Plum Tree Branches

西施与扇子的传说

西施是中国古代四大美女之一，在她的故乡——诸暨有这样一段传说。

传说当年范蠡为寻访贤人，来到诸暨，与正在溪边浣纱的西施相遇。两人一见钟情，便定下百年之好。无奈范蠡国事在身不可久留，次日即要返回都城。在离别的当夜，西施用麦田中的麦秸编成扇子，还用丝线在扇面上绣上了自己的模样，送给范蠡。范蠡明白西施的心意，将扇子带在身上返回了国都。每日他看到扇子就会想起远在诸暨的西施。

有一天这把扇子被越王勾践看到了，他看到西施如此美丽，就打算将她献给吴国国王。无奈，两个本应该在一起的恋人就这样被拆散了。后来，在诸暨农村就有了这样一个风俗：如果姑娘与小伙子相爱了，在夏季来临之时，小伙子就会收到一柄姑娘亲手制作的精美的扇子。

Legend of Xi Shi and Her Fan

Xi Shi was considered one of the four most beautiful women in ancient China. There was a folktale about her in her hometown Zhu Ji.

According to the legend, Fan Li, a court official in the late Spring and Autumn Period (770 B.C. -476 B.C.) came to Zhu Ji to recruit intelligent men for the imperial court. He met Xi Shi at the river side. They fell in love immediately and decided to get married. But Fan Li was on a business trip and had to go back to the capital. The night before he left, Xi Shi wove wheat straws into a fan and embroidered her own portrait on the fan with silk threads. She gave the fan to Fan Li, who understood her feelings. He brought the fan with him to the capital and whenever he saw the fan he thought about Xi Shi in Zhu Ji.

One day King Gou Jian of State Yue saw the fan with the portrait of beautiful Xi Shi. He decided to give her as a concubine to King of State Wu. The two lovers were thus separated forever. From then on, in villages of Zhu Ji when a young woman fell in love with a young man, the young man would receive a beautiful fan personally made by the young woman upon the arrival of summer.

● 西施范蠡相见图
Meeting of Xi Shi and Fan Li

在中国的岭南地区有十月送扇的习俗。因为岭南地区有一个饮食风俗，就是喜好在冬天的时候吃馄饨。由于当地常年高温，因此即使是在冬季吃馄饨也要扇扇子，故当地流传着"把扇吃馄饨"的谚语。但是在中国台湾，将扇子作为礼物送人被认为是一件不吉利的事情。因为在他们的方言中"扇"与"散"读音相同，送扇子就代表着分别和离散，很不吉利。

古时候，葬礼中也用扇子。当时凡是有亲人去世的家庭，都会在门口挂一把白色的扇子，以告知其他人，家中有丧事。

此外，不同职业的人在使用扇子时也有很多规矩。比如，相声演员在表演过程中，扇子虽能作为各种道具使用，但是唯一不能用来扇风，因为如果用扇子扇风就会让观众有很热的感觉，影响观众情绪。

In the south of China some areas have a tradition of giving fans as gifts in October. People in these areas like to have a wonton soup in the winter. It's always hot there all year long, so people have to use fans to cool themselves while eating wonton soup, hence the saying "eating wonton while faning yourself". But in Taiwan, China, it is considered very unlucky to give a fan as a present because in their local dialect, fan sounds similar to parting and separation.

In ancient times, fans were used in funerals, too. A white fan would be hung outside of the home where a person died to inform others that this family was going to have a funeral.

Different professions have different rules about using fans. For example, cross talk actors can only use fans as props, not for cooling purposes. The reason is that if the actor used the fan to cool himself people in the audience might feel hot, which may affect the audience's emotions.

中国扇之最

　　中国现存最大最古老的折扇——明代朱瞻基所作的《松下读书图》折扇。此扇扇骨长82厘米，扇面长59.5厘米，宽152厘米。

　　中国迄今最大的折扇——王星记扇厂生产的《西湖全景图》折扇，扇子边长2.6米，展开有十几平方米，重16公斤。

　　中国最早的全面论述扇子的专著——清代王廷鼎的《杖扇新录》。

Some Bests of Chinese Fans

The biggest and oldest folding fan existing in China today is the folding fan with the *Reading Under a Pine Tree* painting by Zhu Zhanji of the Ming Dynasty. The fan sticks are 82 centimeters long with a fan leaf 59.5 centimeters in length and 152 centimeters in width.

The biggest folding fan as of today in China is the Westlake Panorama Fan produced by Wang Xing Fan Factory. The fan side length is 2.6 meters and the fan leaf area is of over a dozen square meters. It weighs 16 kilograms.

The earliest book with the comprehensive descriptions of fans is the *New Book on Ceremonial Fans* by Wang Tingding of the Qing Dynasty.

- 清代吴昌硕牡丹折扇
Folding Fan with Peony Painting by Wu Changshuo of the Qing Dynasty (1616-1911)